Getting sorted!

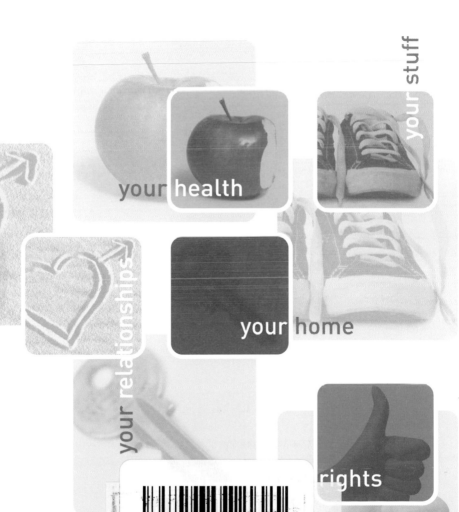

your health

your stuff

your relationships

your home

rights

Published by
British Association for Adoption & Fostering
(BAAF)
Saffron House
6-10 Kirby Street
London EC1N 8TS
www.baaf.org.uk

Charity registration 275689

British Library Cataloguing in Publication Data
A catalogue record for this book is available from the British Library

ISBN 1 903699 95 9

Written by Rebecca Davidson
Project management by Shaila Shah, Director of Publications, BAAF
Illustrations by Fran Orford
Designed by Andrew Haig & Associates
Printed in Great Britain by The Lavenham Press
Trade distribution by Turnaround Publisher Services, Unit 3, Olympia
Trading Estate, Coburg Road, London N22 6TZ

BAAF is the leading UK-wide membership organisation for all those
concerned with adoption, fostering and child care issues.

Acknowledgements

The initial idea for this publication and the text were commissioned and sponsored by Woodside Fostercare, who are delighted with the subsequent development which has led to this guide.

The text for this guide was written by Rebecca Davidson with input from Henrietta Bond.

We would like to thank Marion Hundleby, JoAnne Salmon and her colleagues at Fostering People, Nottingham, and Samina Akhtar at A National Voice for reading and commenting on the text. Thanks also to Larry, Barry and Danny for offering useful suggestions on the illustrations.

Note about the author

Rebecca Davidson worked for several years as Support Services Co-ordinator for an independent foster care association, with responsibility for co-ordinating and overseeing therapy and education provision. She currently specialises in working with people with special educational needs, in particular those with autism and Asperger Syndrome.

Note about the illustrator

The cartoons in this book were drawn by Fran Orford. Fran's cartoons have been used in over 70 magazines and newspapers in both the UK and abroad, including *The Observer*, *Private Eye* and *The Telegraph*. Before becoming a cartoonist Fran set up and ran a Leaving Care Team for NCH in Halifax, West Yorkshire, and before that he worked with homeless and disadvantaged teenagers in London.

Contents

Introduction

Preparing to move on

Becoming an adult is one of the biggest steps we take in our lives. The time between being a young person and becoming an adult is often called "transition" which means a journey or a crossing from one place to another. This book will help you prepare for this journey so that you can arrive at the other side ready to live as an independent adult, and to become the person you really want to be.

Being a teenager isn't easy, and if you've also spent time in care you may feel that you've had more than your fair share of difficult experiences. Hopefully you've also had people to help and support you. It's important that you think about the different choices you can make and the effect these will have on your life, so you can get the best out of your future. As you move from being a teenager into adulthood, you have the right to receive help and support to make good choices.

How to use this book

Only you can make sure you get to where you really want to go in life. Your local authority can give you the support to point you in the right direction. People like teachers, social workers, carers and Connexions Advisers will give you advice to help you along the way. But you are the one becoming the adult and only you can decide how to use the help and support that is offered to you. This is an exciting time in your life, but it may feel a bit scary too – that's why you need to plan ahead.

Think of this book as a bit like a map. When you first take a journey you need to know the names of the different roads and the different places to look out for, otherwise you may get a bit lost and have problems reaching your destination. So you may need to spend a bit of time reading the map. But if you do the journey several times you will find that you learn the way by yourself. You probably won't need the map every time. But it may be useful to have it in your bag or your pocket so you can check it when you need to. So treat this book as a travel companion, a mate you can call upon when you need to.

And whatever you do, remember that no journey worth making is ever straightforward. Maybe you'll take a few wrong turns or find that someone has put a "diversion" sign in the middle of your road. But no matter what has gone wrong before, you don't have to give up or turn back. You can take control of your life and move on. The best travellers are those who learn from their mistakes, check the signs and set off in a new direction.

What you can expect

If you are a young person leaving care, you are entitled to some services and your local authority should make sure that you continue to receive support. The law in England and Wales says that, if you are between the ages of 16 and 21, you should be 'prepared for ceasing to be looked after' (ceasing is another word for ending or finishing). Similar laws are being introduced in Scotland and Northern Ireland. Your local authority must 'advise, assist and befriend' you in order to promote your welfare in the future.

Getting help

Your Personal Adviser

The Children (Leaving Care) Act 2000 says that your local authority should provide you with a Personal Adviser. This person is responsible for assessing your needs (which means working out the kind of support you would need) and deciding what advice, help and support they should give you to help you prepare for the future. As part of this, your Personal Adviser will work with you to prepare a Pathway Plan.

Your Pathway Plan will map out what your needs are and how they will be met. It will include where you are going to live and your plans for education or training or getting a job. The Plan will also say when the local authority thinks you will no longer need support from them or your Personal Adviser.

Your Personal Adviser will also know about grants and financial support that will help you when you are setting up your home or need things for college or your job. They will apply for these on your behalf.

Your local authority also has some financial responsibility for you. You can get extra help with a number of things which are listed later on in this guide. You can always ask your Personal Adviser who will tell you what they are, explain what you can and can't get, and help get the payments for you.

Connexions

Connexions is a government service for all young people aged 13–19, living in England. Each young person has their own Connexions Adviser. This person is usually introduced to them at school or through colleges or drop-in services.

Your Connexions Adviser gives you advice to help you make the journey into adulthood and working life. Connexions works with other organisations to make sure you have a range of opportunities to choose from when you are planning for your future. They can also give you help and advice about issues such as drug abuse, sexual health and homelessness – if you need this. Your Connexions Adviser can also help you identify problems which are stopping you from getting the best out of your education or training. They can put you in touch with special support services who can give you the extra help you need.

Mentors

Some young people leaving care receive help from a mentor. If you think this is something that would help you, you should ask your Personal Adviser or Connexions Adviser if you are "eligible". ("Eligible" means that you fit the rules used to decide if somebody should receive a benefit or service.)

A mentor is someone who:

- **Gets to know you as an individual**
- **Spends a couple of hours with you each week (or fortnight)**
- **Is there for you – you get one-to-one time with your mentor**
- **Listens and doesn't judge you**
- **Is a volunteer**
- **Isn't part of social services, so what they know about you is what you choose to tell them**

Many mentors for young people leaving care are recruited by the Prince's Trust. The Prince's Trust forms partnerships with local organisations who train and supervise mentors who are paired up with local young people leaving care.

Mentors can help you in lots of ways. They can:

- **Give you individual time and attention**

- **Give you advice and encouragement**

- **Provide opportunities for you to learn new skills**

- **Help you find other sources of support**

- **Help you increase your self-esteem and self-confidence**

- **Make you feel that someone is there for you, so you feel less isolated**

- **Help you access grants and programmes provided by the Prince's Trust**

Getting Sorted and *Getting More Sorted*

This guide gives you some tips on how to look after yourself and your things. Obviously, it can only give you a little bit of information, but it does tell you where to go and find out more. There is another book which is like a companion guide to this one, called *Getting More Sorted*. It does cover some of the information in this book, but also discusses other things, like getting into further education, how to prepare for the world of work, moving into your own place, managing your money, and other things besides.

We hope that these books will help you get to where you want to be.

Looking after yourself

Feeling good about yourself

IN THIS SECTION:

In an ideal world I'd like to be...me! Wouldn't it be great if we always felt like that about ourselves? Sadly, most of us spend too much time wishing we were someone else, or wishing that we were thinner, taller, fitter, more confident...We just don't spend enough time appreciating who we are.

Sometimes – especially when things aren't going too well in your life – it's easy to spend your time thinking about the things you don't like about yourself. You may have one of those days where you find yourself asking: 'Why does everything always go wrong for me?' And then you start giving yourself silly answers like: 'It's probably because I'm such a horrible person.' This will just get you down even more, which is why it's very important to learn to feel good about yourself.

Be kind to yourself

Here's some things that can help you feel good about yourself:

- **Focus on the things you like about yourself, e.g. you have a great smile, you are really creative, you have beautiful eyes, you're brilliant with babies, you're the best at computer games, animals love you...**

- **Think about the things other people like about you, e.g. you're a very good listener, you're a kind and loyal friend, you're someone people turn to when they're in trouble, you're good at making people laugh...**

- **When you catch yourself thinking or saying things like 'I'm useless' or 'I hate my body', sit yourself down and give yourself a good telling off! Nobody has the right to be so horrid to you.**

- **If there are things you really don't like about yourself – like your bad temper – think about how you can get help to change them.**

- **Don't expect things to change overnight. If you want to get fitter, become calmer, give up smoking, or jog every day, don't beat yourself up every time something goes wrong. Just dust yourself down and try again.**

- **Praise yourself when you achieve something. It doesn't have to be something big (not screaming your head off when a spider comes up through the bath plughole definitely counts!).**

- Don't spend time with people who drag you down. Friends who always criticise you or make you feel bad about yourself aren't real friends. Move on.

- Don't compare yourself with others – especially not superstars, international footballers or models in adverts. (Do you know that many adverts and pictures in magazines are "touched up" to make the person appear slimmer, sexier, or, if they're a guy, have great pecs and a six-pack?)

- If you're going to have a role model, choose someone who inspires you to make the best of yourself.

- Be kind to yourself when you're having a bad day. If you failed an exam or your dog just died, it's OK to snuggle up under the duvet and watch DVDs.

- Aspirations are good – but impossible dreams are very depressing. Try to have some realistic dreams you have a good chance of achieving.

HELPFUL HINT

Some of the most "confident" people like actors, television presenters and politicians feel very nervous inside – they just don't show it on the outside.

Being "confident" is a trick which you can learn. Act confident even when you don't feel it. If you *act* confident, people will treat you as if you *are* confident. It then doesn't matter how nervous you feel inside because other people can't see this. The more you practise acting confident, the more natural it will become.

Be the type of person other people like

This doesn't mean you have to be the most attractive, the most popular or the funniest person in the world. There are ways of being a really likeable person which will make you feel good about yourself.

In this book we have included lots of tips on getting along with people. Here are some ways to develop these skills:

- If you treat other people the way you'd like to be treated, they are much more likely to treat you well too.

- Being warm and friendly goes a long way. Smile!

- Forget being cool all the time. Learn to laugh at yourself.

- Don't show off. It can also be good to admit your mistakes. People like someone who says, 'You know, I was wrong about that...' much more than someone who has to be right all the time.

- Really listen to other people, especially when they are upset. Find ways to show you understand what they are saying, e.g. 'I can see you really miss her – that must be very hard for you.'

- Show other people how much you value them. This can be by doing something like sending them an e-card or making them a little present, or just giving them a hug and saying, 'You're a great mate to have.'

> ## HELPFUL HINT
>
> **If you want your friends to listen to you, then be prepared to listen to them too. If you've spent the last hour moaning that your boyfriend/girlfriend doesn't listen to you, it's now time to stop and ask your friend, 'So how are you?' And listen to them properly. Don't start talking about yourself again after two minutes!**

Look after your appearance

Whatever your shape or size, you'll always feel better about yourself if you take trouble with your appearance.

- Have regular baths or showers

- Wash and brush your hair regularly

- Wash your face

- Scrub your nails

- Clean your teeth at least twice a day

- Use a good deodorant
- Wash your clothes and change them often
- Wear clean underwear every day
- Clean your shoes
- Put odour-eaters in your trainers
- Check yourself in the mirror before you go out

When you choose what to wear, think about what you're doing and where you're going. You'll feel better about yourself if you're not sticking out like a sore thumb.

- Do you need to be smart for an interview or meeting?
- Will you be getting dirty or doing manual work, so you need to wear old clothes or things that wash easily?
- Will it be hot? You don't want to end up smelly and sweaty!
- Will it be cold? Do you need gloves, a scarf and a warm coat?
- Will you get wet? Do you have something waterproof? Will you need a change of clothes?

HELPFUL HINT

Shoes matter! Don't spoil an interview suit by turning up in trainers. Borrow some shoes from a friend if you don't have any yourself. Make sure they are clean. And don't wear high heels if you have to walk a lot – they could get very uncomfortable.

Get help if you feel put down

If you are feeling put down by others – or constantly putting yourself down – you need to get some help. You don't deserve to feel like this.

Perhaps you are being bullied, picked on or getting racial abuse. Maybe things have happened to you in the past like physical or emotional abuse, which are making you feel bad about yourself. If things like this are getting to you, it's very important not to bottle them up inside.

Talk to the people who are closest to you about how you are feeling. But make sure you choose people you can rely on to keep what you say confidential. Choose people you know will respond in a helpful way and not make you feel worse. Don't choose someone who you know will say 'pull yourself together'. That isn't the kind of advice you need right now!

● **Ask your Personal Adviser, teacher, foster carer, social worker or Connexions Adviser if they know any organisations that can give you advice and support.**

● **Look in your local phone directory under things like Charitable organisations, Voluntary organisations and Youth organisations – you should find relevant organisations in your local area.**

● **Look on the internet for organisations that can help.**

● **Contact your local Citizens Advice Bureau (CAB) for information on who can help you.**

● **Go and see your GP, especially if you are feeling really depressed. Most GP surgeries have counsellors whom you can see.**

Tomorrow is another day

The best thing about life is that we have constant chances to start again. The old 'tomorrow is another day/tomorrow is the first day of the rest of your life' cliché gets said over and over again – because it's true. And it's why we talked about maps at the start of this guide – because if you take a wrong turning you might get lost for a bit, but then you find a new road and head off in a new direction. So even if things haven't gone that well for you in the past, you can always start again. And if today doesn't go that great – well, there's always tomorrow. And next week. And next year.

This is your life!

It's your life and only you can live it. You have as much right to an enjoyable, happy and fulfilling life as anyone else. Do the best you can today and try to make sure tomorrow is even better – but don't put off living because you're waiting for everything to be perfect. It never will be – because life's like that!

So don't forget to take care of yourself and the other people you come across on your journey. And make sure you enjoy yourself as you go. You may never get to the place you meant to reach, but you can do lots of enjoyable and interesting things along the way. And the place you end up in may be better than anywhere you'd ever imagined.

Remember – life is precious and so are you.

Looking after your health

IN THIS SECTION:

Are older people always going on about how important it is to look after your health? It can be a bit boring to hear this again and again, but health is one of the most important things we have. If you neglect or damage your health you will lose out on many good things. You will also make life a lot harder for yourself. If you visit people in hospital take a look around you – aren't you glad it's not you in the bed with lots of tubes hanging out of you? Keep it that way if you possibly can.

Registering with a GP

Everyone should be registered with a GP (doctor) to obtain general health care. If you're not, you need to do the following:

1 **Find out where your nearest GP surgeries are.**

2 **Ask around to see if there are surgeries that people recommend.**

3 **Find their phone number in the phone directory or on the internet, or call in and ask if they have a place for you. If they do not have a place, they can put you on a waiting list.**

4 **If you have been put on a waiting list, make sure you know how long it will be before a place comes up. If the list is a long one, keep looking for somewhere else.**

5 **When you find a surgery and they have a place for you, you will be asked to attend a medical with a nurse and complete an application form. The form is used to keep your basic details together, such as your name, address, date of birth and National Insurance number. Make sure you have as much of this information with you as possible. A foster carer may have a carer-held health record about you. If so, you can show this to your GP. It would also be useful for your GP to be told of who your previous GP was, so that they can make sure that they have up-to-date medical records for you. The medical examination at the GP's surgery may include measuring your weight, height and blood pressure. As well as being asked about any health concerns, you will probably be asked whether you smoke or drink and whether you are having a sexual relationship. Everyone who joins a doctor's surgery gets asked these questions.**

If you're under 16 an adult may need to register you.

Health care is provided free through the NHS. You will not be asked to pay to see a doctor or be treated in a hospital, unless you go to a "private" doctor or want treatment that is not paid for by the NHS.

GP surgeries have something called an "out of hours" service for people who are ill when the surgery is not open. **You should only use this if you feel really unwell and you cannot wait until the surgery opens.** Ring the surgery number. There will probably be an answerphone message giving you an emergency number to call, or you may be asked to leave a message and someone will call you back (see Health Emergencies – later in this chapter).

Registering with a dentist

Follow steps 1 to 4 above of registering with a GP.

You will still be asked to give some information/fill in a form but you will not have a "medical". You may get a "check up" instead.

When you register with a dentist it only lasts for 15 months. If you do not go to the dentist during this time your registration may run out.

Dental treatment isn't free in the same way that NHS treatment is free. Some dentists only treat people who can pay for the service. But generally:

- **If you are under 18 you will get free dental treatment**
- **If you are under 19 and in full-time education you will get free dental treatment**
- **People on benefits like Income Support or Job Seekers Allowance get free dental treatment**
- **Other people on low incomes may also be able to get dental treatment more cheaply**

In an emergency (when you can't wait until the dentist's surgery opens) ring the surgery number. There will probably be an answerphone message giving you an emergency number to call, or you may be asked to leave a message and someone will call you back.

If you are not registered with a dentist you can call NHS Direct on 0845 46 47.

> ## HELPFUL HINT
>
> **If you are frightened of going to the dentist, tell the dentist this. If the dentist knows you are frightened they can often do things to help you relax. There are also things they can do to make it easier for you, like doing one filling at a time rather than several fillings in one go.**

Going to the opticians

Don't neglect your eyesight – If you think that you can't see as well as you should, get your eyes tested.

A list of opticians in your area can be obtained from the Eye Care Trust (0845 129 5001) or local Yellow Pages, etc, and every high street will have a number of opticians shops.

If you do need glasses, the NHS range is cheaper. Remember you don't have to buy your glasses from the optician who tested your eyes, but you will need a copy of your prescription – look around for the best deal. If you choose to have contact lenses you will have to pay for them yourself, so again, shop around and don't forget they are easy to lose, so insure them.

Health emergencies

- If you or someone else is seriously ill or badly hurt call 999 and ask for an ambulance. (DO NOT CALL 999 UNLESS ABSOLUTELY NECESSARY.)

- If you or someone else needs to go to hospital but can get there in a car or taxi, call a taxi or ask someone for a lift.

- If you are worried about yourself or someone else, but don't know if you need to go to hospital, call the NHS Direct 24-hour helpline on 0845 46 47. They will ask you for details of the illness or injury and advise you on what you need to do. Sometimes the person you speak to will take some details and get somebody else to call you back.

- Many places now have an NHS "walk in" centre run by nurses. You don't need to make an appointment. This can be a good place

to start if someone isn't very well but it isn't so serious that they
need to go straight to hospital.

HELPFUL HINT

**If someone has taken an overdose, don't wait! Dial 999
straight away. Follow any instructions you are given. Acting
quickly can save someone's life.**

Getting a prescription

Your doctor may give you a prescription for medicine or for things like
asthma inhalers.

You need to do the following:

● Ask where you can get the medicine from. Your GP or the GP's
receptionist will be able to tell you where the nearest pharmacy
(chemist) is.

● If you are not sure what the prescription is for, ask your GP
before you collect it.

● You will be asked at the pharmacy whether you will be paying for
your prescription. If you are not sure, on the back of the
prescription it tells you who needs to pay and who doesn't. Your
pharmacist will also be able to help you with this.

● You may have to wait for your prescription to be made up, so ask
how long it will take and either wait or arrange to call back later.

● Some prescriptions can be collected straight from your GP. Your
GP should tell you if this is the case.

If you have a medical condition

You may have a medical condition such as diabetes, asthma or
eczema. It is important that you understand how to manage your
condition, so that you can keep yourself healthy.

This may include:

1   How to keep medications safely, e.g. you may need to keep some medications in the fridge.

2   How to use medications safely, e.g. what dose you need to take and how often you should take it.

3   If you need to inject any medicines or use things like inhalers, make sure you know how to do this safely and effectively. If you haven't done something for a while and can't remember how to do it, ask to be shown again.

4   Make sure you know when to seek help.

Your medical records

Your GP will have notes and records about your medical history. This will include the results of any medical tests and appointments your GP has referred you to, e.g. with a hospital or specialist. Your notes will also contain details of the "diagnosis" (description of symptoms) of any medical condition that you may have. Your GP will be able to tell you more about this.

It is your right to be able to see your medical records, but you will have to make an appointment with your GP. (In some very rare cases a doctor may hold back information if they think it will cause "serious harm" for a person to see part of their medical records.)

Preparing for an appointment

Going to see a doctor, nurse, specialist, or therapist can be worrying, especially if what you are going to talk about is sensitive or personal.

To help you prepare for the appointment:

● Write down any questions you want to ask before you go

● Write down any answers you are given when you are there

● Take someone with you for support if you want to

● If you don't understand, ask for the information to be explained again

● Try not to get too embarrassed about things – everyone has to get advice from time to time

Drugs, solvents, alcohol and cigarettes

We know you're going 'Oh no – here comes the lecture' but drugs – which include solvents, cigarettes and alcohol – can seriously screw up your life.

Get wise about drugs. Don't believe everything your friends tell you. There are useful websites and helplines where you can get the full facts.

Drugs

People take drugs for a lot of reasons, some medical and some social.

Some drugs are legal, such as alcohol and cigarettes, and some are illegal, such as dope, coke, ecstasy and smack.

Although drugs can make you feel better for a short while, the effects wear off and can leave you feeling anxious, depressed and messed up. In extreme cases drugs can kill.

Other risks include:

● **Getting caught in possession of illegal drugs**

● **Mood swings and being unable to function properly in your daily life**

● **Infections from sharing needles**

● **You can get addicted**

● **Your habit will cost you a lot of money**

● **Risks to your unborn child**

The best advice is – don't start in the first place. But if you have a drugs problem then seek help. Talk to someone you trust, visit your GP or call a confidential helpline. You won't be reported to the police for seeking help.

Solvents

Sniffing solvents is **very dangerous.** You are at risk of:

- suffocation
- poisoning
- choking on your vomit
- death

Like any drug, the feeling you get from sniffing solvents soon wears off. You will then feel much worse than you did before.

THE SHORT-TERM EFFECTS ARE NOT WORTH THE RISK AND CAN DO YOU LASTING HARM.

Alcohol

Alcohol is a drug as it stops you from functioning properly. You can also get addicted to it.

A small amount of alcohol in a social situation, such as at a party or when you're out with your mates is fine, but drinking a lot of alcohol can seriously damage your health and prevent you from functioning properly.

Do you know what the recommended "units" of alcohol are for men and women? At the time we wrote this guide it was 14 for women and 21 for men – in a whole week! Do you know that a "unit" is not the same as a glass? Some drinks like spirits and cocktails contain 2 or more units per drink.

The limit doesn't mean that it is healthy or safe to drink that amount every week. To keep really healthy you should try and drink no more than 5–10 units whether you are a man or woman. And try to make sure you have at least one day a week when you don't drink any alcohol.

➥ MEL'S STORY

For my cousin's hen party we planned this mad night. We started with a pub crawl and then hit a club. In the club they were selling doubles of vodka half price. We all had our tongues hanging out, we were that thirsty from dancing. The thing with vodka is that it goes down so easy. I don't remember how I got to the hospital. I do remember that stomach pump thing though. It was disgusting. But the worse thing was I couldn't fly to Spain with everyone the next day. So I missed the wedding. I can't look at vodka now. Just the smell of it makes me throw up.

HELPFUL HINT

It's not OK to "save up" all your units of alcohol for one day. "Binge drinking" is extremely bad for you. You can get alcohol poisoning from drinking too much in one go, which can kill you or cause permanent damage to your brain.

If you think someone has alcohol poisoning – don't wait. Seek urgent medical help.

Smoking

If you smoke you are at risk from:

● lung cancer

● bronchitis

● heart disease

● early death

Reasons for giving up smoking:

● You can never be totally healthy if you smoke – however much you exercise

● Smoking affects the way you perform – true athletes don't smoke

● You spend lots of money you could use for other things

- Your breath smells – so does your hair, your clothes and things like your sheets

- Smoking affects other people's health – they breathe in your smoke (which can seriously harm them)

- Smoking while pregnant can seriously harm your unborn baby

- You run the risk of getting serious illnesses like cancer and heart disease

- Most smokers don't live as long as other people

- If you get a disease caused by smoking your treatment costs the NHS a lot of money. This money could be used to help people who have health problems they didn't cause by smoking!

- Smoking affects so many people. How would you explain to your partner or your child that you are going to die because you have a disease caused by smoking?

Giving up smoking

We know it isn't easy but it's an incredibly worthwhile thing to do. However, unless you really want to give up smoking, you may not succeed. You will need a lot of support if you decide to give up. Call a helpline or go to your GP to find out what help is available.

The best thing to do is:

- Decide on a start date when you are not stressed or under pressure

- Make sure you stick to this date!

- Think about the money you will save and how much healthier you will be

- When you would normally smoke, think about what you will do instead

- If you do have a cigarette, don't give in! Just stop again and keep trying to stay away from cigarettes.

- Take one day at a time. Every day without a cigarette is a success in itself.

Useful organisations

Talk to Frank and **The National Drugs Helpline** offer lots of down-to-earth information and advice about drugs. Call 0800 776 600, or look at www.ndh.org.uk. All help is confidential and they're open 24 hours a day.

Drugscope gives safety advice about drugs. Visit their website at www.drugscope.org.uk.

ADFAM offers confidential support for families and friends of drug users, and helpful written information. Call their National Helpline on 020 7928 8900, email them at admin@adfam.orq.uk or look at www.adfam.org.uk.

Alateen and **Al-Anon** are 24-hour services for young people who think they have a drinking problem or are worried about someone close to them. Their 24-hour helpline is 020 7403 0888.

Look in the Yellow Pages under "A" for your local branch of **Alcoholics Anonymous**.

Quit is the charity for people who want to stop smoking. You can call their helpline on 0800 002200, visit their website at www.quit.org.uk or email them for personal help on stopsmokinq@quit.orq.uk.

Planning and preparing meals

IN THIS SECTION:

There's so much talk about food these days: eat this, it's good for you. But don't eat too much of that! Eat five portions of fruit and veg and cut down on fat! Eat more fish and less meat! It's no wonder people get confused and have more hang-ups about food than almost anything else you can think of!

Food is something good. It gives you "fuel" – that's energy and nutrition. But it's also there to be enjoyed. When people want to celebrate, one of the first things they think about is, 'what shall we eat?' Food also says something about who we are. Vegetarians choose not to eat meat and fish. Vegans don't eat any foods which come from animals, such as milk and butter. Food also says something about our culture and our customs. Food plays a big part in many religious celebrations. Recipes are also passed down through families and communities. Knowing how to cook certain dishes gives people a sense of who they are and where they belong and sharing delicious dishes with your friends is a fun thing to do together!

Enjoy your food

Here are some reasons why it's worth making the effort to find out about food.

● **Enjoying a meal with other people is a great way to make friends**

● **Trying out new flavours and ways of preparing food is fun**

● **Making a special cake or a meal for someone is a great way to say thank you or to show them you care**

● **You can get a real sense of achievement from preparing and cooking your own food**

● **Learning to cook food saves you lots of money. A meal made with fresh ingredients is usually a lot cheaper than a ready-made microwave meal or getting a take-away.**

● **If you cook your own food, you know what's in it! You can cut out all that extra salt and sugar that's in ready-made foods.**

● **Learning to cook certain foods can help you feel part of your own community and culture**

Basic food facts

As they say, here's the science bit...

Food is full of vitamins and minerals which make our bodies work. Every organ in your body – that's things like your heart, lungs, kidneys, and even your skin, hair and teeth – needs the right foods to keep it working properly.

The only way to keep yourself healthy and have a really fit body is to eat a "balanced" diet – this means eating foods that are good for you, and eating a variety of foods from each of the four food groups shown on the next page.

Eating lots of fatty, sugary and salty foods, such as burgers, chips, chocolate and fizzy drinks, is bad for your body. These foods don't have the vitamins and minerals in them that you need. They can also clog up your arteries which means that the blood can't pump around your body properly.

Not eating enough food is also bad for you. It weakens your organs and your skeleton. Making yourself throw up food is also harmful for your body.

If you're not eating right you may notice some of these things happening to your body:

● **Feeling tired and having no energy**

● **Feeling depressed**

● **Feeling unwell and being more likely to catch colds and other illnesses**

● **Getting spots**

● **Lank and lifeless hair**

● **Putting on too much weight**

● **Losing too much weight**

● **Feeling dizzy**

● **Your periods stopping (girls) because you're not eating enough**

In the long run, if you continue to eat badly you put yourself at risk of illnesses such as cancer and heart attacks. If you think you may have a problem with food like eating too little (anorexia nervosa) or making yourself throw up (bulimia nervosa), or eating too much (binge/compulsive eating) you should get some help. Talk to your doctor or to someone you trust. There are also helpful websites you can look at.

Now for some more facts to help you make the right food choices.

There are four main food groups:

1 **Milk and dairy products**

2 **Proteins – meat, fish, beans, nuts, lentils**

3 **Fruit and vegetables**

4 **Carbohydrates – bread, pasta, rice, cereal**

HELPFUL HINT

Make sure you choose a variety of things from *each* of the four food groups *every* day for a healthy, balanced diet. Have a well-stocked fridge and cupboard and save money – by planning ahead.

- Think about the meals you will eat during the week ahead. Can you buy food and cook with other people? Buying in bulk is often cheaper than buying for just one person.

- Always make a list of what you need before you go. Cross off anything that is not essential. If you have some money left at the end, you can decide whether you have enough for a treat.

- Work out how much money you have to spend. Don't forget *ALL* of the things you need your money to cover.

- Look at the prices of each item. Supermarket own-brands are often the cheapest.

- Check the "sell by" date and "use by" date. Make sure you don't end up wasting anything because you can't use it in time. You can often find that things with a later sell-by date are stacked further back on supermarket shelves – look out for these.

- Try and do one big shop from a supermarket or market. Buying bits and pieces from corner shops and garage shops can be very expensive.

- Don't buy lots of frozen food if you don't have freezer space to store it.

HELPFUL HINTS

Use-by dates: For foods like meat, fish and eggs and ready-made meals, it's very important to follow use-by dates so you don't get food poisoning. But some foods like fresh fruit, vegetables and bread are often OK to use for a few days after their use-by dates. If fruit, vegetables or bread look and smell fresh and healthy, they're probably still OK. If they're turning strange colours or growing mould, throw them away!

- See what you have got in the cupboards, fridge and freezer. Do you have the right combination of things to make a filling, healthy meal?

- Think about the *four food groups* above. Do you have things to eat from at least two of them, three if possible?

- If you are a bit short of food, is there anything you could buy to add to what you've already got so that you can make a meal? Maybe some vegetables, pasta, meat or bread.

- Enjoy your food but don't pick your favourite things every time. Try lots of different recipes and experiment with new foods so you get a healthy combination.

Following a recipe

- Before you start, read what ingredients you need and what bowls, pans and tools you will need. Get them all out ready for when you need them.

- Choose a recipe that you will feel happy with and enjoy making. Don't go for something too difficult to start with. Simple food made well always tastes great.

- If there is something you need and haven't got, write it down and note how much you need so you can get it before you start cooking.

- Check whether there is anything else you need to do beforehand, e.g. defrosting something, or heating the oven or "marinating" something (this means putting something like meat or fish in a sauce to soak up the flavour, before you cook it).

- Read each step of the recipe very carefully. Make sure you do exactly what it says. Take your time and concentrate.

- If you don't know how to do something, phone a friend or ask a housemate.

Using the cooker rings

There are usually four rings on the top of your cooker – two for large saucepans and two for small saucepans.

Gas rings come on straight away. Electric rings can take a while to heat up and cool down. Be patient!

Each ring has its own control switch. As a guideline:

0   Off

1–2   To keep something simmering

3   To keep something boiling safely

4–6   To bring food to the boil but needs to be turned down to 3 when it reaches boiling point

Using the oven

There are two main kinds of ovens:

1 **Gas ovens, which may need to be lit when you turn them on**

2 **Electric ovens, which can either be fan-assisted or conventional**

When you cook in an oven, you need to heat the oven up first to the right temperature **before** you put the food in to cook.

You will usually find instructions for how to cook foods on the packaging the food comes in or in the recipe you are following. **Always follow these instructions. And make sure you turn the oven off when you have finished cooking!**

Microwaves

Microwave ovens can be easy to use, but some have quite complicated instructions. Read these instructions carefully or ask someone to show you how to use the oven.

To cook in a microwave you need to set the temperature you need the food to cook at and the length of time the food needs to cook for, and then press the **START** button.

You cannot cook some foods in a microwave, for example, pizza – this needs to go into an oven so it can "crisp up". Always check the instructions.

Microwaves can be good for re-heating food, but always make sure the food is piping hot before you eat it.

EVERY KITCHEN SHOULD HAVE A FIRE BLANKET AND FIRE EXTINGUISHER SUITABLE FOR PUTTING OUT ELECTRICAL OR GAS FIRES.

Setting the table

If you've decided to cook a meal for friends, you will need to set the table so that everyone can be comfortable while eating. How you do this will depend on the answers to the following questions.

1   HOW MANY people are eating and drinking?

2   WHAT will you be eating and drinking?

3   WILL the food already be on the plates or in serving dishes?

So what do you need to do?

1   Cover the table with a cloth or mats so that the heat from hot food or any spilt food doesn't damage the table

2   Think about what you are eating and what cutlery (knives, forks, spoons) you will need. If you are eating more than one course, you will need enough cutlery for each course.

3   Think about what crockery you will need, for example, plates, dishes, serving dishes, glasses, cups

Here's a simple place setting.

Putting away leftover food

If you have leftover food, think carefully before you throw it away. Check whether there is enough food to make a snack or another meal.

- Don't leave leftover food in a warm place such as in the sun or in a saucepan which is left out. This is when harmful germs can grow on it and make you very ill if you eat the leftovers.

- Make sure the food is *cold* before putting it into containers such as plastic boxes, bags or on a plate or bowl covered in clingfilm or foil

- Store food in the fridge

- Don't forget it's there. Eat it within two days.

 WARREN'S STORY

My foster mum was not what you call a good cook. Lovely lady but the same thing every week – sausages on Monday, patties on Tuesday, fish on Friday, that kind of thing. I watch all those cooking programmes on the telly and I thought, you know food can be better than that. And my granddaddy was a cook. As a kid I loved his stuff – rice and peas and curry goat and all that. So I got these books out of the library, and I found some recipes on the internet. Now I cook this big meal for everyone on Friday nights. Everyone asks their mates round, cos my food is just so tasty!

Useful organisations

www.Lifebytes.gov.uk has information about all sorts of useful things. Their section on healthy eating gives easy-to-follow straightforward info.

The British Nutrition Foundation website, www.nutrition.org.uk, has lots of info on food and healthy eating.

If you or someone you know has a problem with eating – such as eating too little (anorexia nervosa) or eating too much (binge eating), or throwing up after eating (bulimia nervosa), **The Eating Disorders Association** can help. Their young people's helpline number is 01603 765050. You can visit their website on www.edauk.com.

www.Childline.org.uk has a useful section on eating problems.

Relationships and sexual health

TOM HAD BEEN TOLD TO ALWAYS WEAR
A CONDOM...

IN THIS SECTION:

Relationships should be happy experiences which make you feel good abut yourself. Sex may be part of this but it should only happen when you are ready for it.

Sexuality is about more than having sex. Your sexuality is an important part of who you are as a person and how you relate to other people. It includes being heterosexual (straight), homosexual (gay or lesbian) or bisexual (attracted to both men and women). Celebrate your sexuality by finding out about your body and how it works, and how to keep yourself safe and healthy by being in control.

Be in control

- Don't have sex just because you think everyone else is doing it. Only do it if it's right for you.

- Celibacy (making a decision not to have sex) can be cool. Some people choose this because of religious beliefs but some choose it because they like the feeling of being in control of their own bodies.

- Having full sex isn't the only way to be "intimate" with someone.

- Sex isn't always like it's shown on television or in the movies. Sometimes it can be even better! But it can also be disappointing, painful or embarrassing if you're not really ready for it.

- If you're having sex to please someone else, e.g. your boyfriend/girlfriend or as a dare, you're probably not going to enjoy it very much.

- If someone doesn't respect your wishes not to have sex, then dump them!

- It's a bit of a cliché but the best things in life are usually the things it's worth waiting for. Sex can be fantastic and it's worth waiting for the right person, the right time and the right place.

- If there are things that are worrying you about sex (maybe you've had a bad experience in the past) don't try and pretend it's all OK. Find someone you can talk to such as your doctor, a counsellor or your foster carer.

- If you are too embarrassed to talk to your doctor or a sexual health adviser, then go online. There are websites with lots of straightforward advice and some have counsellors you can email in strict confidence.

● And remember that "unprotected" sex, i.e. without using a condom, can lead to a pregnancy or a sexually transmitted disease (STD).

Sexual identity

Some of us like members of the opposite sex, some of us like people of the same sex. Some of us like both. It's really that simple.

Don't let other people tease or bully you about your sexuality, or stop you from being who you are. Talk to someone you trust if you are suffering this kind of discrimination. There are also helplines and support groups for young people who are "coming out" i.e. telling people and identifying that they are lesbian, gay or bisexual.

Doing it for yourself

Masturbation (often referred to as "wanking") is normal. It is not "dirty" or "disgusting". It's a natural part of exploring your own sexuality. It can also be safer than having sex with someone else.

Be safe

● Find out about the different types of contraception and protection available. How effective are they against unwanted pregnancy, sexually transmitted diseases (STDs) and HIV?

● Make sure you always take responsibility for your own contraception and protection against STDs and HIV – and don't rely on or believe that someone else has it covered just because they tell you that they will do this.

● Never have unprotected sex just because someone else says it will be OK.

● Think about the situations you are putting yourself in. How well do you know the people you are with? Should you go to someone's house if you don't know them? If you're not sure, don't go.

- If you do decide to go home with a stranger, make sure someone knows where you are. And make sure the person you are going home with knows that someone else knows.

- If you start to have sex and then change your mind, tell the other person that you don't want sex and you want to stop. It's your body and you don't have to do anything you don't want to.

- Think about how much you are drinking. Stay sober enough to make sensible decisions. You don't want to wake up and find you've had unprotected sex with someone you don't know or like.

- Do you know what you are drinking? Sometimes people put drugs or spirits into someone's drink so they can rape them later. Your drink won't look any different if it's been tampered with. Don't accept a drink from a stranger unless you've watched the drink being poured by the bar staff.

Unprotected sex

If you've had unprotected sex – whether it's with a male or female, in a straight or gay sexual experience – you need to do the following:

- Make an appointment at your GP surgery or health clinic to have a check up for STDs.

- If you're a girl and have sex with a boy, get emergency contraception. This can be obtained from pharmacists, health clinics and GP surgeries.

➡ LIAM'S STORY

When I was 13, I was that desperate to "do it". I went with this older girl from year 6. Then I did it with loads and loads of girls. I didn't like any of them much but I thought I was cool. At college I met my best mate, Mike. He told me he didn't do it until he was 17. He did it with this girl he was crazy about. She was the only girl he'd ever slept with. I laughed at him a bit and called him a "virgin". But he didn't care. You could see from the way he talked that his first time had been amazing. Inside I felt quite jealous cos it's never been that good for me.

Rape and sexual assault

If you've been raped

Rape is when someone forces you into having sex when you don't want to. It can happen to men as well as women. If you've been raped you need to contact the police. Don't wash or change your clothes as they can be used for evidence. The police will ask you to have a medical examination so they can use evidence from the rape to bring charges against the person who has raped you.

The medical examiner who carries out this examination will be used to working with people who have been through very distressing situations. They will do their best to make you comfortable. The police will also try to give you as much support as possible and put you in touch with other organisations that can give you specialist support.

You have a right to refuse this medical examination. But if you do, the police may not have enough evidence to bring charges against the person who raped you.

You should also follow the steps (see previous page) on emergency contraception and getting checks for sexually transmitted diseases (STDs).

Sexual assaults

Any type of situation where you are forced to perform or be involved in a sexual act which you don't want to take part in is a crime. Follow the steps above for contacting the police if this happens to you.

HELPFUL HINT

You should never feel ashamed about being raped, sexually abused or assaulted. Being raped, abused or assaulted is the same as being attacked. People do it to hurt you and show their power over you. They want you to feel small and helpless. Don't let them win by making you feel like this. The person who should feel ashamed is the person who commits an act of rape or sexually abuses or assaults somebody.

Protection/contraception

When you are in a sexual relationship, you need to think carefully about protection.

There are two main reasons for using contraception:

1   To stop an unwanted pregnancy (if you're in a straight relationship)

2   To prevent you catching and passing on sexually transmitted diseases (STDs) and HIV (if you're in a straight or gay relationship)

You need to discuss with your partner what contraception you will use.

For women there are a range of options, e.g. the pill, cap/coil or implant, etc.

For men, it's the condom (also called a rubber, sheath, johnny, etc).

It is best to talk to your GP or family planning clinic to find out more and decide what will suit you. They will be able to give you information about how reliable a particular contraception is, how to use it properly and how it will affect your body.

Withdrawing (the man pulling his penis out of the woman's vagina just before he comes) is not a reliable method of contraception. Neither is trying to guess when in a month a woman won't be fertile (as part of her monthly cycle) and so won't get pregnant. Neither of these "methods" protects you safely from getting pregnant – nor do they protect you from STDs and HIV.

Make sure you always have a method of contraception ready for when you might need it. Never rely on being able to get hold of emergency contraception at short notice. **Be prepared.**

Sexually transmitted diseases (STDs)

Sexually transmitted diseases (STDs), sometimes known as VD (venereal diseases), are diseases caught by having sex with an affected person. **Diseases include: gonorrhoea, syphilis and herpes.**

You are more at risk if you don't use contraception, or you or your partner have had sexual relationships with several other people.

Symptoms include:

● **Itching and discharge from your sexual organs**

● **Sores on your sexual organs**

● **Pain, especially when you pee**

● **Possible sores in your mouth**

In some cases one of the partners (often the woman) may not have any symptoms and may not know they have this disease until their partner is diagnosed.

Sometimes you may have these symptoms (which haven't been caused by having sex) but still need to get them treated straight away.

If you have these symptoms, or have just found out that your partner (or a previous partner) has been diagnosed with an STD, make an appointment or go to the drop-in service at your GP, health centre or your local STD clinic.

You should stop having sex until you have had a medical check-up and taken advice from your GP/STD clinic. You should tell your partner so that they can have a check up also.

HIV and AIDS

What are HIV and AIDS?

AIDS (Acquired Immune Deficiency Syndrome) is thought to be caused by a virus known as HIV. This means that the body's natural defences break down and can't fight infection.

Not everyone who gets HIV goes on to develop AIDS.

These days some people prefer not to use the term AIDS. They use the term "HIV plus" for someone who has developed Acquired Immune Deficiency Syndrome. This is because some people have stupid ideas about AIDS – and some people who are labelled as having AIDS have been treated badly. You **do not** get HIV/AIDS from being with people who have AIDS, using the same toilet as them or drinking from the same cups or glasses! People with HIV and AIDS need the chance to live as normal a life as possible and be supported and accepted by others.

HIV is passed on through bodily fluids – blood, semen and vaginal fluid. The most common way of catching HIV is through unprotected sex – whether it's oral, vaginal or anal.

People in straight (male/female) relationships have the same risk of getting HIV as people who are gay or bisexual.

Sharing needles when taking drugs also puts you at risk. Having body piercings and tattoos can also be a risk if the equipment isn't properly sterilised.

Some people are born with HIV, which they inherit from their parents.

How to avoid HIV and AIDS

- **Don't rush into having sex with someone you don't know**
- **Always practise safe sex – use a condom**
- **Don't share needles**
- **If you are having a body piercing or tattoos, go somewhere where equipment is sterilised**
- **If you are worried, seek advice**

HIV is a serious infection and it's important to avoid it if you can. However, this doesn't mean that it's the end of the world for everyone who gets it. These days fewer and fewer people die as a result of getting HIV/AIDS. Support and medicine are available to help people who have the condition keep as healthy as possible and make the best of their lives.

Pregnancy

If you think you might be pregnant you should get a pregnancy test done right away either at your GP surgery or local reproductive and sexual health clinic. Don't rely on a home pregnancy kit. Reproductive and sexual health clinics offer free and confidential advice and support on all issues relating to sexual health. This includes contraception, condoms and lubricants, check-ups for sexually transmitted infections, smear tests, pregnancy tests, abortion referrals and referrals to other services which can support you.

If you didn't plan to get pregnant, you probably need to do some careful thinking. You should talk about it with your partner and someone that you trust. There are local services that can give you advice and support to help you think through the decisions you need to make.

Making these decisions can be very difficult but you mustn't put them off. The longer you leave it the more chance there is that some of these options will no longer be available to you. There are legal limits after which a baby cannot be aborted. The later the abortion the more health risks there are for you.

Your options are:

- **To keep the baby**
- **For the baby to be raised by a member of your family or your partner's family**
- **To have the baby adopted**
- **To have an abortion**

Think very carefully about all these options and what they mean to you – both now and in the future. Don't let anyone force you into a situation you are not happy with or one that you know you will regret.

Useful organisations

A beginner's guide to coming out can be found on the www.Channel4.com website under the "life" section. This includes lots of valuable info, including details of how to contact other support services.

There are helplines, support groups (and some youth groups) for gay, lesbian and bisexual people in many parts of the UK. Check on the internet or through Yellow Pages.

A famous helpline is the **London Lesbian & Gay Switchboard**, which gives 24-hour advice and support on 020 7837 7324.

The Albert Kennedy Trust works to make sure that lesbian, gay and bisexual people live in accepting, caring situations and don't face discrimination. They run schemes to find foster carers, supported lodgings and specialist housing for young people who need somewhere safe and supportive to live. Visit their website at www.akt.org.uk.

The Terrence Higgins Trust offers information and advice to women and men in England and Wales affected by HIV and AIDS. Contact their helpline on 0845 122 1200 or visit them at www.tht.org.uk.

Brook Advisory Centre gives information and advice on issues like contraception, pregnancy and STDs. It can be contacted on its helpline on 0800 018 5023 or call "Ask Brook" (for under 19s) on 0800 292930, or visit www.brook.org.uk.

Visit **www.RapeCrisis.org.uk** for advice, information and details of your local Rape Crisis Centre. You can also try the Yellow Pages under 'R' for details of local centres.

The **FPA** (previously called the **Family Planning Association**) has lots of helpful advice on its website at www.fpa.org.uk. You can phone their UK helpline on 0845 310 1334, or look in the Yellow Pages to find your local family planning clinic.

Getting out and about

IN THIS SECTION:

1 **What's going on in your neighbourhood?**
2 **Using public transport**
3 **Planning an outing**
4 **Planning a party**

Getting out there is important, if you're going to find out what's on offer. Whether it's seeing live bands, getting cut-price cinema tickets or chances to meet new people – you won't find most of these just by sitting indoors.

What's going on in your neighbourhood?

Here are some hints for finding out what's going on in your area.

- **Go along to your local library – they should have lots of info about clubs and events. This may include things to do when you haven't got much money or things that are free.**

- **Look at notice boards in youth clubs or on the internet – you may find details of a local sports club, dance class or gym.**

- **Look in shop windows – they often have adverts for local clubs and events.**

- **Ask your local leisure centre for their brochure of what's on – they often do an all-in-one booklet for six months ahead. Does the leisure centre do cheap rates at certain times? Are you entitled to a "leisure card" or free entry to leisure services? Ask your Connexions Adviser or Personal Adviser or the social worker from the Leaving Care team to find out and help you get it.**

- **Do you fancy a bit of drama? Is there a drama class in your area? Maybe you want to join a band. Look out for notices or do an internet search for this in your area.**

- **Is there a local street fair or festival coming up? There's often free food to try and the atmosphere is great.**

- **Find out when your local cinema does special offers – many cinemas have a half price night, two-for-one tickets or cheaper matinee sessions. Some even have a free viewing of new films – for people who book early.**

➡ SHANE'S STORY

At school I thought poetry was rubbish. Then I went on this workshop where they did drama and music. I went for the music. But the music workshop was all booked up. This tutor said to me, 'Come to the poetry. It'll be good.' I thought no, that's not my thing. But it was brilliant! One of the best things I ever did. At the end we got to read our poems out. Me and this girl, we both did poems about our lives, about growing up in care. She read hers and I read mine. I looked out and saw that people in the audience were crying. I write poems all the time now. It's a good way to get your feelings down, especially if you're feeling mad.

Using public transport

If you are going somewhere and you can't walk there or use a bicycle, public transport may be the best idea – for example, this could be using a bus, tube, tram, taxi, or train.

Things to think about:

● Which sort of transport will be the cheapest?

● Which will take you nearest to where you want to go?

● How long will it take?

● Do you have a timetable so you can work out times and places to leave from?

● How much will it cost?

● Will you have to change bus, train, tram, tube or taxi on your journey?

● Can you travel "off peak" to save money? If you travel outside busy times (like morning and evening rush hour) it's usually cheaper. You can sometimes get an all-day pass which allows you to make as many journeys as you like in one day.

Getting a bus/train pass is often the cheapest way to travel, especially if you travel every day. This could be a monthly or weekly pass, or maybe you can get a loan from your college or work for a yearly pass.

Ask your social worker, Personal Adviser or Connexions Adviser whether there are schemes to help young people buy travel cards.

Taking a taxi

Taxis are a lot safer than walking home in the dark alone. But when you get into a car with a total stranger you can put yourself at risk (men and women). Follow these basic tips for your protection.

Safety tips:

- **Only black cabs can be "hailed" (asked to take you as a passenger) in the street. Any other cars looking for fares are illegal – and possibly dangerous.**

- **Always use a registered taxi or minicab**

- **Keep the number of a taxi or minicab firm you trust with you**

- **Try and book your taxi beforehand. When you phone up ask for the name of the driver, the make and colour of the car. Check this when it arrives.**

- **Try to travel with a friend**

- **Always sit in the back seat**

- **If you feel threatened go with your instincts – tell the driver to stop in a busy place and get out of the car**

- **If the driver won't stop, then shout and wave out of the window. Use your mobile to call the police.**

- **Never be tempted to use an unlicensed taxi or minicab – you might be robbed, raped or attacked**

Ordering a taxi by phone

1 **Try to use a taxi firm that you have used before or one that has been recommended by someone you know. In some places there are women-only taxis with women drivers.**

2 **Make sure you have enough money to pay for the journey. If in doubt, ask on the phone how much it is likely to be.**

3 **Keep a note of the number of the taxi firm you've just called**

4 **If the taxi doesn't turn up on time, ring and ask (politely) how much longer it is likely to be**

5   Follow the safety tips above

6   Don't forget to pay before you get out of the taxi

7   Say 'thank you'

8   Often people tip taxi drivers but you should only do this if you can afford it and feel that they have given you a good service. A tip is usually quite a small amount. The person will appreciate it no matter how big or small.

9   If the driver is rude or drives very badly, don't tip and don't use that service again. Find one you feel happy with.

10 Be polite and keep on good terms with your chosen taxi service. At busy times taxi firms are more likely to send a taxi for customers they like.

Planning an outing

An outing can be something like:

● A trip to the local park

● A night out on the town

● A visit to a big theme park

When you are planning an outing think about:

● Who is going?

● Where are you going? Will everyone enjoy it?

● Have you asked them what they would like to do?

● How many people are going? Do they all know each other or will they be meeting each other for the first time?

● How will you travel? Can you walk? Do you need to use public transport? Do you have a timetable? How long will the journey take?

● Have you checked the opening/closing hours of the place you are going to? How long will you stay?

● Will you buy food there or will it be better to take food and drinks with you? Maybe everyone could bring something for a picnic.

- Try not to take alcohol – it's banned from lots of public places. You also don't want someone getting really drunk and spoiling everyone's day.

- What sort of clothes do you need? Will you need flat shoes and waterproofs?

- How much will it cost for food, travel and admissions? Do you need to save up for a while?

> **HELPFUL HINT**
>
> Always make sure everyone can get home safely, especially at night. If you are likely to be back late, make some plans for people to share taxis or get lifts together, or for friends to stay over at each other's places.

Planning a party

Parties are good fun and everyone loves a good party! Here's some things to think about.

- What sort of party? A small one in your house or a big one in a community hall?

- If it's in your house, are the other people who live in your house OK with this? What about the neighbours?

- If it's a big party, who is going to pay for renting the venue, e.g. community hall, club, room above the pub?

- Maybe you can hire somewhere as a group. You can all put in a set amount of money and each invite a certain number of friends.

- Find out the limit on how many people the venue (pub/club/hall) can take. Most places have a strict fire safety limit. If you ask too many people then some of them may get turned away.

- Do you need to supply food and drink, or does the venue have its own licensed bar and catering service? Check out the costs of any extras, like food, before you book anywhere.

● If you're supplying your own food, it's a good idea to make a list of everything you need, and then buy in bulk from the local cash and carry.

● If you're having the party on your own, can you get some friends to make or bring a few things?

● Do you need to order anything in advance? Many supermarkets do ready-made birthday cakes, but if you want something really special, you may need to order this a week or so before.

● Leave plenty of time to get everything ready.

● Make sure you tell the neighbours that there will be a party and there may be a bit of noise. You could always invite them to join you!

● It's not a good idea to let people drink too much. And doing drugs at a party... forget it! Someone could get very ill and if the police get involved, there'll be trouble.

● Be reasonable. If the venue closes at midnight encourage your guests to leave then. If your party is at home then be thoughtful. Your neighbours may put up with some noise until midnight but they won't appreciate someone turning up the music at 3am.

● Make sure to budget if you need to buy a present or a card. Even a small gift or home-made card shows that you have put in some thought.

● Thank people who have helped you with the party.

HELPFUL HINT

If your party has caused a nuisance to any of your neighbours, go and apologise, or drop a little note through their door. An apology in time can stop a small problem turning into a big problem.

2

Caring for your clothes

The way we look says a lot about us. Someone who is clean and well turned out generally looks and feels more confident. Someone whose clothes are dirty and smelly isn't going to impress anyone, especially if you're going for an interview or a date.

If you're wearing casual clothes like jeans and a T-shirt you still want them to look and smell fresh – even if they're full of designer holes.

Using a washing machine

The easiest way to wash clothes (and bedding and towels) is in a washing machine. You might have a washing machine in your home, or you might need to go to a launderette.

Using washing machines at a launderette

At a launderette you pay to use the washing machines. These are usually much bigger than a washing machine at home. There is usually someone there to show you how to use the machines.

At the launderette you can also pay to use a tumble dryer which will dry your clothes for you (see section on tumble dryers).

> **HELPFUL HINT**
>
> **Make sure you have a supply of loose change to use at the launderette. Most machines use 20p pieces and £1.00 coins.**
>
> **You will need to take your own washing powder with you.**

All clothes and bedding have symbols on the label that tell you what temperature they need to be washed at and how you should care for them.

| HANDWASH ONLY | MACHINE WASH NORMAL | MACHINE WASH COLD | MACHINE WASH 50° | DO NOT WASH |

Before you start, ask someone to show you how to use the washing machine. Make sure that you really understand how to do it before you try it on your own.

Easy steps to using a washing machine

1 Sort your clothes and bedding into piles of dark colours, light colours, wool, and delicate things

2 Check that all the labels on the clothes and bedding in each pile have the same symbol or temperature written on them

3 Choose a pile and put it in the washing machine, making sure the machine is empty first

4 Look at the washing powder/liquid packaging. Does it need to go in the drawer at the top of the washing machine, or straight in with the washing? Measure out the amount you need by following the instructions.

5 Look at the symbols and temperatures written on the washing machine next to the controls. Find the one that matches the symbols on your clothes.

6 Use the controls to switch the washing machine onto this washing "cycle"

HELPFUL HINTS

● Don't put your clothes on any old washing cycle just because you don't know how to set the machine. Your clothes may never look the same again!

● Make sure to take everything out of the pockets before you put things in the wash.

 BEZ'S STORY

My mate, Nathan, brought all his washing around and we took it down the launderette. There were all these people there and we waited, like, hours for a machine. Nathan said it would be OK to shove everything in together. We could go down the shops while it was washing. He said to put it on a really hot wash cos some of his stuff was dead manky. When we got back it was like a disaster area. My tracksuit bottoms were all shrunk and funny. And there was this white shirt I needed for my interview at college. It had gone pink.

Hand-washing clothes

If you do not have a washing machine, or cannot get to a launderette, you will have to hand-wash your clothes and bedding.

Some clothes have to be washed by hand because they are too delicate to be washed and spun in the washing machine.

Easy steps to hand-washing

1   Fill up a bowl or clean sink with hot water. Make sure it's not too hot to put your hands in safely. (Use warm water if you are washing delicate clothes.)

2   Add a little washing powder or liquid to the water. If you add too much you won't be able to rinse it out!

3   Put the clothes and bedding in the water and leave them to soak for 5–10 minutes, then give them a wash by rubbing them between your hands in the water.

4   Check to see if any stains or marks are coming out. If not, you may need to work on that part until the stain goes.

5   Take the clothes and bedding out of the water and wring the water out (be gentle with delicate clothes). Put the clothes on the draining board or in another bowl.

6   Rinse the bowl out and fill with clean warm water. Rinse the clothes in this water.

7   Keep changing the water until there are no soap bubbles coming out of the clothes.

8   Wring the water out of the clothes and bedding (remember delicate things need gentle handling).

Hanging the washing out

Clothes and bedding dry best outside on a washing line in good weather. A hot, sunny day or a dry, breezy day are perfect for this. They smell fresh and dry and have fewer creases so they are easier to iron!

If the weather is bad, hang your clothes and bedding on a drying frame indoors. (You can get wire drying frames – sometimes called "clothes horses" – from pound shops and large supermarkets.) Try to spread the clothes and bed linen out as much as possible. Stand the drying frame a short distance away from a radiator – make sure that the clothes are not touching it because they may scorch or burn.

If you have a tumble dryer you could use this.

Tumble drying

Some washing machines are also tumble dryers, but some tumble dryers are separate machines that look very much like a washing machine.

If you don't have a tumble dryer at home and want to dry your clothes quickly you could take them to a launderette and use a tumble dryer there, but remember this costs money.

Tumble dryers are not suitable for all clothes as they use very hot temperatures to dry the clothes and bedding and "tumble" it around in the machine.

The symbols below show whether an item can or cannot be tumble dried, and which heat setting they should be on.

CAN BE TUMBLE DRIED

TUMBLE DRY ON HIGH HEAT

TUMBLE DRY ON LOW HEAT

DO NOT TUMBLE DRY

Dry cleaning

Some clothes cannot be washed in a washing machine or by hand-washing. They need to go to a dry cleaners, because the fabric they are made of is very delicate. Dry cleaners use chemicals to clean clothes instead of soap and water. Dry cleaning is expensive, so you may want to check the labels in clothes before you buy them.

The following symbols mean **DRY CLEAN ONLY** and **DO NOT DRY CLEAN**

DRY CLEAN ONLY

DO NOT DRY CLEAN

Ironing

It is important that you use the iron with care so you don't burn yourself, your clothes, or anything else around you!

It is best to use an ironing board, but if you do not have one, then fold a thick towel in half and place it on a hard surface such as a table or kitchen worktop.

You need to make sure the iron is set to the right temperature for your clothes. It will say on the label in your clothes what fabric they are made of and whether they can be ironed with a cool or hot iron.

These are the symbols you need to look for:

| COOL | WARM | HOT | DO NOT IRON |

HELPFUL HINTS

● When you need to put the iron down, stand it on the flat surface at the back of the iron (the bit behind your hand). This does not get hot. Don't rest it on its bottom – it will burn things.

● Never walk away from an iron when it is switched on. A child, animal or even another adult may get badly hurt.

Basic sewing and mending

The most common types of sewing and mending you may need to do are:

● Mending hems (round the bottom of trouser legs and skirts)

● Sewing buttons on

● Mending a tear in your clothes

Threading a needle

1 Unravel a length of cotton from the cotton reel. Don't make this too long – the length between your elbow and hand is probably about right.

2 Cut the length of cotton. Make sure it is a clean cut so you have an un-frayed edge. This will make it easier to get it through the eye of the needle.

3 Hold the needle in the light where you can see the eye clearly. Thread the cotton through – it helps if you have steady hands!

4 Once the cotton has been threaded onto the needle, make sure you pull a few centimetres of cotton through so it doesn't come unthreaded.

5 Hold the eye of the needle while you sew.

Sewing on a button

1 Place the button where you need it.

2 With the needle and thread, sew in and out of the holes in the button by pushing the needle from the back of the fabric through to the front of the fabric – and then back through a different hole to the back again.

3 Repeat this until the button is secure.

4 Sew a few stitches through the back of the fabric so the end of the thread doesn't pull out. Cut the end of the thread.

HELPFUL HINT

To knot or not to knot? Some people tie a knot in the end of the cotton before they start sewing. Some people prefer to make a few stitches in the back of the material when they start – so the stitches stop the end of the cotton from pulling through the button. Find out what works best for you.

Using Wonderweb to mend a hem

Wonderweb is a thin strip of fabric which, when you place it between two pieces of material and iron it, "bonds" (joins) them together securely. It is much easier than sewing and can be bought at most supermarkets. Always read the instructions carefully.

3

Getting connected

IN THIS SECTION:

1 **Buying a mobile phone**
2 **If your phone doesn't work**
3 **Your rights and your mobile**

If you read all the computer and gadget magazines you may not need this chapter. But you might also find some useful advice on what to do if your mobile stops working just after you buy it.

Buying a mobile phone

If you buy a mobile phone there are several things you need to think about. You need to make sure that you get:

● **The right phone for you**

● **The best price**

● **The right contract**

● **The right coverage**

Go to a mobile phone shop which sells phones made by different companies. Tell the sales assistant what sort of phone you are looking for and how you want to use it. Get them to suggest a range of different phones and contracts that will be the best value for you. Some supermarkets also sell phones and it's worth checking what they can offer. You might also find special deals on the internet – but check the contract details very carefully.

Don't rush into a decision. Get plenty of information on the choices available and take it away to look at before you make a decision. Ask friends and people you know who have a mobile.

These are the key things to think about when you buy a mobile:

1 *Coverage* – does the network you want have good coverage in your area? Some phone companies have poor reception in some parts of the country.

2 *Power* – how long will your phone last before it needs recharging? The flashiest looking phone isn't much good if it keeps running out of charge. Compare minimum "talk times" between different phones.

3 *Usability* – is the phone easy to use and comfortable to hold? Flashy phones aren't always the easiest to use.

4 *Doing the right things* – not all phones do the same things in the same way, e.g. some don't save messages, or delete texts if you can't send them straight away. Which services matter most to you?

5 *Don't pay for what you don't need* – do you really need a camera or video phone? If you don't – or if you think the temptation to use it will cost you too much – don't buy one.

6 *Don't pay too much* – prices vary from store to store so shop around. And remember you'll pay over the odds for the latest phones. New phones are launched every few months, so in six months time the phone you really like will probably be cheaper.

7 *The right deal* – pay-as-you-go can be the best deal because you don't have to pay rental. But it can also be more expensive because the calls can cost more than rental deals. (If you are under 18 you will probably be restricted to pay-as-you-go unless a responsible adult is willing to take a contract out for you.)

8 *Are you a heavy texter?* If so, look for deals that allow you to buy text bundles at cheap prices.

If your phone doesn't work

If you have a problem with the mobile you have bought you need to check the following things:

● Check there really is a fault and that the problem is not caused by user error (you using it wrongly), an accident, or just normal wear and tear

● If possible, collect together all the paperwork for your phone and check the details/instructions before you make the complaint (this can save embarrassment)

● You will need to contact the place where you bought the phone to report the problem and find out what they will do about it

● If the fault is with the phone, you should contact the shop where you bought it

● If the fault is with the network or SIM card, you need to contact your service provider (the company which provides the phone service)

➡ LEAH'S STORY

I got offered this phone as a free upgrade. It was dead cute. But I got so I hated it that much I would've thrown it out the window. Where I live there is bad coverage. I'd be, like, halfway through a call and the phone would cut off. So I'd try and send a text but if I was on the bus or something it would go wrong. The text wouldn't go through and it would disappear. It used to make me so mad. I complained several times but they didn't do anything. In the shop they said it wasn't their fault because the phone was made by another company. I should've read the contract properly. In the end I moved to another company when my contract ran out. It's much better. I wouldn't have one of those tiny phones again.

Your rights and your mobile

The law says that if you buy a mobile, it must be:

● **of satisfactory quality**

● **fit for its purpose**

● **as described in the literature (that's the stuff written in the advertising leaflets)**

If you buy a phone and find that it doesn't do some or all of these things, you have rights.

Your rights and the phone

If you have only had the phone a few weeks or haven't had enough time to check it, you are probably entitled to a refund for a fault or because it was poorly described, or you may be able to request a replacement.

If the fault is only minor (something small) and is easily put right, it is reasonable to accept a repair. If this repair is not satisfactory, you should then be able to ask for a replacement or refund.

If you have had the phone longer than a few weeks, you will probably still be entitled to a repair or replacement carried out within a reasonable period of time after you bought it. If this repair is not OK, you should be entitled to a replacement or refund.

If the phone can't be repaired or replaced economically you are entitled to a refund. The trader may make a reduction (take some money away) from the price you paid for the use you have already had from the phone.

If you are out of pocket in any other way, you may be entitled to compensation over and above the price of the phone.

If you are entitled to a replacement or a refund, the trader has to arrange this and can't tell you to go back to the manufacturer.

Your rights and the network

When you buy a phone, you need to be connected to a network in order to use it. You may do this by having a line rental contract or by buying pay-as-you-go vouchers. When you take out this contract or buy these vouchers, you are entering into a contract with the "service provider" (the company which provides the connection). If there are problems, you may be entitled to a refund or compensation.

You need to remember the following things.

- Always read the terms and conditions of your contract carefully.

- You usually have seven working days to cancel a contract if you do change your mind (but not always – check this carefully). After that time you have no right to cancel the service simply because you change your mind.

- If you choose a contract phone rather than a pay-as-you-go-phone, you will be committed to using a certain network, at a certain tariff (rate), for a minimum length of time.

- You have no rights to repairs, refunds or replacements if you have not used or looked after your phone in line with any instructions, e.g. if you drop it in the bath you won't get it replaced by the shop!

- Wear and tear caused by your use of the phone is not counted as a fault. If you get dust or water in the phone, or jam the keys by pressing them too hard, that is your problem.

- Your rights cannot be taken away by terms and conditions written into a notice, receipt, contract, warranty or guarantee.

Unfortunately, it's all a bit complicated! If you are having problems understanding your rights or getting a shop to replace faulty goods, it's best to get help. Consumer organisations like the Citizens Advice Bureau can help you.

Getting online

IN THIS SECTION:

Using the internet

What can you use the internet for?

Email

● **Contacting friends and family**

● **Contacting your tutor, social worker, Personal Adviser or Connexions Adviser**

● **Contacting someone from an organisation whose services you might use**

Internet

● **Finding information and advice**

● **Buying stuff**

● **Fun and entertainment**

You may have an internet connection at home. If you don't, you can often use the internet at these places:

● **Your local library**

● **A local voluntary organisation**

● **College**

● **An internet café – although there is a charge for use in these**

What you need

To use either email or the internet, you will need access to a computer that has an internet connection. If you do not have a computer, there may be internet-connected computers that you can use in your local library, a local voluntary organisation, college, an internet café (there is a charge for these) or at a friend's place.

If you have a computer and a landline phone, then you could consider getting an internet connection at home, but you need to think carefully about what this will cost. Are there several of you who could club together to pay for this? If you need this for your work or study, there may be a grant to help you with this – talk to your Connexions or career adviser.

There are several different types of internet connection service available:

- **Dial-up services**

- **Broadband services**

- **Cable services**

Dial-up services use your landline phone to connect to the internet. This means that while you are using the internet you won't be able to use your landline phone. These come in two different types of package – "fixed rental charge", where you pay a fixed amount per month however much you use the internet, and "pay per use", where you are charged for the time you spend on the connection.

Broadband services offer a faster connection which means that you can download music and video, but they can be more expensive. They require the phone company to make changes to the way your phone landline works, so you have to take out a longer contract (usually a year).

Cable services are provided by the companies that provide cable TV services. Usually they offer deals if you sign up for their TV, phone and internet connections together.

The different types of services and costs can be very confusing and it is best to ask someone before you start to pay for something.

- **Ask a friend who knows about computers**

- **Ask at college or the people who run the computer department where you work**

- **Read computer magazines – these may confuse you at first but keep reading and you'll soon pick it up**

- **Check out a local computer users group – they are usually very happy to help**

- **Or why not attend a computer course? Your Connexions Adviser or school or college should be able to sort this out for you**

Email

To use email you need a way of getting onto the internet and a way of sending, reading and replying to messages.

If you have your own computer then you can use an email program to do this or a web-based email service.

If you have to use a computer somewhere else, then you will have to use a web-based service such as Hotmail or Yahoo, but there are also many others. There are advantages to using a web-based email service:

- **You can access it anywhere there are computers connected to the internet**
- **The services are usually free**
- **They're quite easy to sign up for**
- **They can be helpful if you're going away and need to keep in contact with someone**

Email DOs and DON'Ts

Do

- **Keep email messages as short as possible**
- **Think about who you are sending to – what you send to your mates is one thing, but a lot of people use email just like letters and expect things to be clear and well written**
- **Check your spelling and don't use lots of jargon, especially if you are contacting strangers or asking people for help**
- **Read the message and make sure it says what you mean before you send it**

Don't

- **Send nasty messages to people who have turned you down for something**
- **Pass on hoax messages**
- **Use it to harass people**

Exploring on the Web

The Web (or World Wide Web) is what most people mean when they say "the internet". It's a series of connected websites (millions and millions of them). Websites have addresses which you type into the address bar of your internet browser. For example, the Connexions website address is www.connexions.gov.uk.

You can use the Web for:

- **Looking up information**
- **Help with your college work**
- **Checking train times**
- **Finding out information from all over the world**
- **Checking your bank or building society account**
- **Fun – you can download music and videos (be careful if you have a slow connection that you pay for by the minute because a song can take a long time to download)**
- **Buying things, if you have a credit or debit card**
- **Selling things through websites like ebay**

Safety online

The internet is like any other "place". There are people using the internet who want to rip you off and do things that are illegal.

- **If you are looking to buy something from a website, does it have a phone number to call if anything goes wrong? Do you trust the company that runs the site? Look for the secure site symbol.**

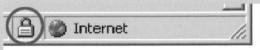

- **Any number of sites offer music for free – in most cases this is illegal. You usually have to pay for music.**
- **Don't give out your contact details unless you really have to – and then only if you trust the people you are giving them to.**
- **Be careful about arranging to meet people you have "met" in chatrooms or on dating sites. You never know who they really are.**

- Only enter financial or personal details into a website if it has a secure address and "padlock" symbol, which show that it is a secure site.

- If something is illegal to buy in the UK, then it's illegal if you buy it from another country over the internet.

Useful organisations

BBC Webwise – www.bbc.co.uk/webwise/ – gives advice on getting started.

UK Online Centres – www.ufi.com/ukol/ – These are public centres where you can learn to use computers and the Internet.
Call free on 0800 771 234.

For info on staying safe online visit **www.getsafeonline.org** and **www.thinkuknow.co.uk**.

Children and young people's charity **NCH** produces its own internet safety guide – visit **www.nch.org.uk** to find out more.

4

Looking after
the house

Living with others

IN THIS SECTION:

You might like to play your music very loudly, invite lots of people around or watch certain programmes on TV. But maybe your foster carers or housemates won't. Small things can turn into big bust-ups if you don't learn to think about other people around you. Compromise is the name of the game when you are living with other people. This means that sometimes you get the things *you* want and sometimes other people get the things *they* want. It's much easier to live in a place where people get along. Don't let a row over whose turn it is to buy a pint of milk turn into World War III.

Many shared houses have some agreed responsibilities (they may be called "house rules") to help everyone live together. If there aren't any, perhaps you could suggest that it might be useful to have some simple ones that everyone discusses and agrees to.

Things to find out in a shared house

These are the kinds of things you need to find out:

- **Is there a cleaning rota?**
- **Who buys cleaning products and toilet rolls?**
- **Do you buy your own food? Do you share things like milk, tea and coffee?**
- **Does everyone cook together or separately?**
- **Do you share the bills and who is in charge of paying them?**
- **Which day does the council collect the rubbish? Who puts the bin bags out for collection?**
- **What about guests and parties? Are they allowed?**
- **What about smoking? Are people allowed to smoke in the house? Remember – it's bad for you!**

How to be an OK person to live with

- **Make sure you do your share of the cleaning and do your washing up – don't leave dirty plates and cups around**
- **Make sure you have the money ready to pay your share of the bills**

- Don't leave your things all over shared areas of the house. Tidy up!

- Think about other people before you play your music loudly. Maybe they are trying to sleep or study.

- Think about other people before you invite friends round or organise a party, especially if it's late in the evening. Tidy up afterwards.

- Make sure you lock doors and windows when you go out

- Knock on other people's bedroom doors before entering

- If you use up the last of the milk, tea or toilet roll, make sure you replace it

HELPFUL HINT

It's important to pay your bills for things like gas, electricity and telephones. If you don't pay on time your service may be cut off. There is usually a charge to reconnect the service. You may also be "blacklisted" by credit companies if you run up debts for services.

Be a good negotiator

Negotiation is a very useful skill to develop, especially when you are living with other people. Being a good negotiator means being able to put your point across and listen to what other people think and feel without things turning into an argument.

Here are some ways to be a good negotiator:

- Suggest everyone sits down to talk about the issue

- Listen carefully to what other people have to say

- Don't get personal, slag other people off or swear at them

- Calmly put your point across – don't raise your voice

- Think about the way you say things. It's OK to say 'I don't agree with you' or 'That's not the way I see it'. It's not OK to say 'You're so wrong' or 'You're stupid!'.

● Look for solutions – don't get bogged down with the problems or whether it's someone's fault. Find a solution everyone can agree on, even if it's not perfect.

● Try hard to stick to the decision the group has made. Don't go off and do your own thing even if you are not keen on the decision.

● It's OK to try out an idea for a week or two and then sit down together again and talk about how things have gone. You might want to change the solution if you can find a better one this time.

➡ MIA'S STORY

When I was younger I was pushed around a lot by other people. These days I know my mind and what I want. I like to live somewhere clean and tidy. I'm fussy about it. When I moved into my new place, the other people there were such scruffs. It made me so mad. I used to tell them I wouldn't put up with it. I wrote a list of rules but no-one followed them. I even got into a fight with one of the girls about it.

My boyfriend told me I was stressing too much. He said I should try and see it from other people's point of view. We had a house meeting and I said what I felt. Other people said what they felt. We came up with some rules everyone said they'd follow. It's not perfect but it works OK. I get less stressed now if someone forgets to wash up.

Getting along with others

One of the best ways to make life easy for yourself is getting on with other people.

If people like you, they will make more effort to help you and be nice to you in return. Even if you don't like someone very much, it's better to try and get along with them – it can save a lot of hassle in the long run.

● Respect other people.

● A friendly smile goes a long way – even if you feel shy inside.

- It's not good to say "please" and "thank you". It can make a big difference to the way people see you.

- Watch your language! Swearing makes some people feel uncomfortable.

- Make an effort with people you don't know. They probably feel as awkward as you do.

- If you don't know what to talk about, ask someone about themselves, e.g. 'What are you studying? or 'Those are great shoes. Where did you get them?'

- If you disagree with someone, put your point across calmly.

- Respect other people's right to their opinion, i.e. what they think. Don't "rubbish" their ideas if you don't agree with them. Just explain why you see things differently.

- Don't get into a fight. Agree to disagree, and if necessary walk away. Discuss it again later when you are both calm.

- Try to pick the right moment to say difficult things. Judge the other person's mood. If your housemate's just been dumped by his girlfriend, it's not the best time to tell him that you think his new jeans are naff!

- Don't assume people will be free to talk about something just because you are. Ask them if they have a few minutes to sit down and have a chat.

- Everyone needs privacy sometimes. Respect other people's privacy, and explain if you need some "time out" for yourself.

CLAUDIA'S STORY

I'm a very private person and I need my space. Sharing a room with this other girl at college almost did my head in. She seemed like she was really stuck up. We got so we didn't speak to each other most of the time. But I found her crying one day and we got chatting. She told me she was missing her friends and she was so lonely. She said she felt like everyone else was confident and having a good time. I told her I felt like that too. We got to be good mates after that. She was a good laugh. We agreed that if either of us needed some space the other one would go down to the TV lounge. Or one of us would go out for a bit.

Taking care of others

If you take care of other people they are more likely to take care of you. Think about the ways your words and actions affect other people.

- **Remember people's birthdays. Even a late card or a quick phone call is better than nothing.**

- **If someone is upset, don't ignore it. Ask if there is anything you can do, and next time you see them ask if they are now OK.**

- **If you haven't seen someone for a while, call round or telephone to find out how they are.**

- **If someone's feeling unwell, ask if there is anything you can get them.**

- **If someone's struggling with something, think about what you could do or say to be helpful and encouraging.**

- **Congratulate other people when they do something well. Everyone needs a bit of praise.**

- **Paying someone a compliment can make their day. They may be worried that their new haircut is a disaster and your words will make them feel a lot better.**

- **If you have to tell someone something you know they don't want to hear, think how you can say it in a way that won't upset them too much. 'You're cool but please don't ring me so early in the morning. I'm a lot lazier than you!'**

Having a house key

Having a house key is an important responsibility. You need to think about the following things.

- **Where are you going to keep your key? On a key ring, on a chain around your neck or attached to a belt loop on your jeans?**

- **Whose house is the key for? Make sure you ask permission before you invite people around.**

- **Just because you've got a key doesn't mean you can let yourself into the house when you are supposed to be somewhere else!**

Pets

Pets can be good companions and some people get lots of pleasure out of looking after animals. But you need to think carefully about the following things before getting a pet.

- Does your housing contract allow you to keep pets? Some contracts ban pets and if you keep one, you will be "in breach" of your contract. You might lose your home if you do this.

- If pets are allowed, does the contract say what sort of pets? A hamster or goldfish may be allowed but dogs and cats may be banned.

- Are the people you live with happy for you to have a pet? Will they help you to look after it?

- Are you sure you will be able to give a pet the care and time it will need?

- Do you have enough space to keep your pet? Even animals like rabbits and guinea pigs need room to run around.

- How much will it cost to buy your pet? Some people re-home cats and dogs from animal rescue centres, but the centre will expect you to show that you can provide a safe, secure home for the animal.

- How much will it cost to look after your pet, e.g. buying food, bedding, cleaning kit, housing? Some pets need annual vaccinations to protect them from diseases.

- What happens if your pet gets ill or is run over? Can you afford vet bills? Some people take out insurance to cover these.

- Who will look after your pet if you are ill or away?

Useful organisations

The RSPCA's website **www.rspca.org.uk** gives advice on caring for different types of pets.

www.allaboutpets.org – the national pet care information service is run by The Blue Cross.

www.bluecross.org.uk – The Blue Cross runs four animal hospitals which give free veterinary care to pets of people on low incomes (although a donation is always appreciated). These hospitals are only in certain parts of the country.

Cleaning your home

IN THIS SECTION:

If you're someone who loves to keep everything around you just perfect, you might not need to read this section. But if you're like most of us – and get a bit messy now and then – you may find some of these tips helpful.

Why it matters

Love it or loathe it, everyone needs to do their share of tidying and cleaning. Most housing contracts say you must keep the place in reasonable order. If you don't, you might get chucked out.

Tidying is important because you will be able to find things when you need them, and it makes it less likely that people will take your things by mistake.

Cleaning is important because dirt, dust and old food create germs that can make you ill, and can trigger asthma and allergies, and a dirty house is not a nice place to invite your friends to. Plus, living in a mess can really get you down.

What you need

To do a good job of cleaning and tidying you need the following.

- **A duster (you can make dusters out of old cotton clothes, such as a worn-out T-shirt)**
- **Furniture polish**
- **Vacuum cleaner/hoover**
- **A floor mop**
- **A dustpan and brush**
- **Multi-purpose cleaner for bathrooms and kitchens. This could be a liquid, cream or spray. Some types of cleaners can't be used on baths or cookers, so read the instructions.**
- **A kitchen cloth**
- **Dustbin bags**
- **Bleach. You might need it if something like a toilet or bath is blocked, or very dirty, but be careful with this as it can burn your skin and stain your clothes. It must never be swallowed so it's**

important not to get it on plates, cutlery, cups and saucepans. Read the instructions!

In lots of houses you will find that things like a vacuum cleaner and mop are already provided, but you may need to buy cleaning sprays and polishes yourself. Supermarket own-brands and items from cut-price stores and markets can be just as good as expensive brands.

Being "green" (environmentally friendly) is good, but it is usually more expensive. If you want to buy environmentally-friendly products you may need to save money on other things.

Cleaning a room

You may only have one room to look after, but if you share a house you will probably need to help with cleaning it all. You might want to work out a rota which tells you whose turn it is to clean a certain part of the house and when.

	MON	TUES	WED	THURS	FRI	SAT	SUN
Kitchen	Amy	Mike	Nita	Jamal	Kyle	Denise	Jo
Bathroom	Mike	Nita	Jamal	Kyle	Denise	Jo	Amy
Living room	Nita	Jamal	Kyle	Denise	Jo	Amy	Mike
Hallway	Jamal	Kyle	Denise	Jo	Amy	Mike	Nita

Cleaning your bedroom

1 Pick up everything from the floor and put it away where it belongs. Don't stuff it in cupboards or under the bed!

2 Clear every surface by putting away everything you don't need.

3 Take dirty plates, mugs, and glasses to the kitchen and wash them up.

4 Put any dirty clothes in the wash basket.

5 Take your dirty bedding off the bed and put it in the wash basket. Change the bed. Put a clean sheet, duvet cover and pillowcases on the bed.

6 Get a duster and polish and wipe all the surfaces in the room.

7 Vacuum/hoover the whole floor. Move the furniture so you can get under things and into the corners!

Most of these things will be the same when you are cleaning other rooms. Kitchens, bathrooms and toilets are a bit different because they have surfaces which need special cleaning to keep them hygienic.

HELPFUL HINT

You should clean your bedroom and change and wash your bedding every week. Dirty bed linen and stuffy bedrooms smell horrible. It's a real turn-off for visitors!

Cleaning the kitchen

Follow steps 1 and 2 above.

But also:

1 Using warm, soapy water and/or anti-bacterial cleaner and a clean cloth, wipe all the work surfaces and any tables.

2 Make sure the place you are going to stack the washing up is clean.

3 Do the washing up (see our washing up tips later in this chapter).

4 Wash the sink out carefully after you have finished washing up – you may need to use some anti-bacterial cleaner.

5 Clean the cooker and the oven (see next page).

6 Sweep or vacuum the floor and then, if you don't have carpet, mop the floor with clean soapy water or anti-bacterial cleaner. Make sure you don't make the floor too wet, as it will be slippery and dangerous.

Cleaning the fridge

Check the inside of the fridge and make sure nothing has spilt. Wipe any surfaces or shelves with a wet cloth. Don't forget to wipe the outside as well. Chuck out any food that has become rotten or mouldy.

Normally you will only need to clean the fridge out thoroughly every couple of months (unless you spill something or some old food goes rotten and slimy).

1 Take everything out of the fridge.

2 Take out the shelves and soak them in clean warm soapy water and then give them a good scrub with the scouring side of a sponge.

3 Wipe around the inside of the fridge with a clean cloth and warm soapy water/anti-bacterial cleaner, making sure you go right into the corners.

4 Leave the fridge to dry for 5–10 minutes before putting everything back in it.

5 Sort through your food and throw away anything that is past its "sell by" date.

Many new fridges self-defrost but some older ones need de-frosting (letting all the ice melt so it doesn't clog up). Follow the instructions that come with the fridge. You need to put a bowl underneath the fridge to collect the melted ice water. Don't forget to switch the fridge back on!

Cleaning an oven

You will only need to clean your oven every couple of months unless things have spilt when they are cooking. You need to check whether your oven is "self-cleaning" before you start as this means you only need to clean the shelves and the doors. You should not clean the inside of a self-cleaning oven as it has a special surface which cleans itself.

If it is not a self-cleaning oven, you need to:

● Fill the sink (or bath if the sink isn't big enough) with hot, soapy water. Take out the oven shelves and leave them to soak in the water.

● Using an oven cleaning product (or hot water and washing-up liquid), wipe around the inside of the oven. If there are any bits stuck on, carefully use a blunt knife to gently scrape them off.

Cleaning the bathroom

Follow steps 1 and 2 of "Cleaning your bedroom" above and then:

1 Using warm soapy water and/or a bathroom cleaning product, wipe around the sink and bath. Get into all the corners and around the taps. If the taps are dirty and encrusted, use limescale remover to clean them.

2 Pour some bleach around the toilet bowl and leave for a few minutes before scrubbing the bowl with a toilet brush.

3 Using a cloth that is ONLY for the toilet, wipe around the seat and lid of the toilet with warm water and a cleaning product.

4 Sweep or vacuum the bathroom floor. If it's a lino or tiled floor, mop it using warm soapy water.

 JADE'S STORY

The guys in our place never wash up. They're such a pain. But one time – after Kay and me had moaned at them for hours – they said OK. We'll surprise you. And they did. Yeah, it was a really big surprise. They did OK with the plates and they only smashed one glass. But the worst bit was Kay's new wok. Her friend gave it to her for her birthday. The lads had spent ages scrubbing off the non-stick surface. I can tell you Kay was not happy.

Washing up

Are you one of those people who holds a cup under the cold tap and thinks it's washed? If so, you'd better read on!

1 Use a washing up bowl, if you have one, or fill the sink with water if you don't

2 Make sure the water is hot enough to get dishes clean, but not so hot you'll burn your hands!

3 Add a small squeeze of washing-up liquid

4 Wear rubber gloves if you have these

5 Use a washing up brush, dishcloth or J-cloth

6 Put the cutlery (knives, forks, spoons) in the bowl so it can soak while you wash some of the other things

7 Wash glasses first

8 Wash the dirtiest and greasiest items last. It's usually best to wash saucepans and frying pans after you've washed the cups, plates and dishes.

9 If things are not getting clean, then change the water!

10 Make sure you stack things carefully to drain. If something won't fit, dry it up straight away with a tea-towel.

11 When everything is dry, put it away where it belongs

12 Carefully rinse out any cloths or brushes you have used. Don't leave bits of food in them to go rotten!

13 If the tea-towel is very wet, hang it somewhere to dry. Don't forget to wash these regularly.

HELPFUL HINT

Check if your saucepan or frying pan is non-stick. You must not use washing up brushes or scrubbing pads if it is – use a cloth instead.

Basic maintenance

It's important to know how to do some basic mending and maintenance jobs. There are some common jobs like changing a light bulb that you should be able to do safely on your own.

Other household mending and maintenance such as plumbing, electrics and gas repairs will need to be done by an expert.

NEVER ATTEMPT TO DO PLUMBING, ELECTRICAL OR GAS REPAIRS BY YOURSELF.

Changing a light bulb

Easy – but needs to be done safely.

1   Make sure the light switch is OFF. If you're not sure (maybe because there are two switches in a room) get someone to stand by the switch, ready to turn it off.

2   Find something safe to stand on like a solid chair or stepladder.

3   Cover your hand with a tea-towel or cloth and gently take hold of the light bulb. Most bulbs need to be turned anti-clockwise (the other way to the way clock hands turn). Don't grip the bulb tightly or it might break in your fingers. Nasty!

4   Look and see what number of "watts" the old bulb has written on it. Always use the right "wattage" or you could start a fire.

5   Put the old bulb down somewhere safe while you put the new bulb in the socket.

6   Hold the bulb with a cloth, push it gently into the socket and turn it clockwise until it is held there.

7   Switch the light on to see if it works.

8   Wrap the old bulb carefully in something like newspapers, and put it in the bin.

Safety tips

We could write a whole book about safety. But the best advice is to find out all you can from websites and local services. Your council, the fire service, police and gas and electricity company will publish leaflets and advice on their websites.

Here are some very basic tips.

●   Make sure you have a planned escape route in case of fire.

●   If you don't have a fire alarm, think about getting one fitted. You can get them from most DIY stores. Some councils and fire services will put fire alarms into your home for free.

●   Get advice on the best way to put out fires. Some fires – like fires in a chip pan – should never be put out with water.

- The law says that electrical appliances should come with plugs already fitted. It is recommended that people don't change plugs themselves.

- Never stand on anything wobbly or uneven. Never stand on anything if you're not sure it is strong enough to take your weight.

- Make sure stepladders and ladders are fully opened/extended so they balance evenly. Read any instructions that come with them.

- Keep electrical items like hair dryers, curling tongs, electrical razors and electric heaters away from water.

- Don't have trailing wires around the place, as people can trip over them.

- Don't leave candles unattended – they could fall over and start a fire.

- Don't leave heaters close to things like curtains or piles of newspapers – this could start a fire.

- Don't cover radiators and heaters – this could start a fire.

- Use oven gloves or wrap a doubled-up tea-towel around your hands to get hot dishes out of the oven.

Useful organisations

www.direct.gov.uk has some home safety pages in its Home and Community section. This includes things like smoke alarms and planning a fire escape route.

Visit **www.shelter.org.uk** and select the website relevant to the country you live in. They have things like free downloadable factsheets on safety in the home.

Dealing with the rubbish

IN THIS SECTION:

1   **Putting the rubbish out**
2   **Recycling**

This section is about getting your hands dirty!

Putting the rubbish out

It's not the nicest task but someone needs to do it, otherwise you'll end up with smells and will attract mice, rats, flies and ants. Nice!

● **The day before your rubbish is collected, go round the house and empty all the bins into black dustbin bags. Make sure you pick up any rubbish you see lying around.**

● **Make sure you tie the sacks up properly so the rubbish can't fall out!**

● **If you have dustbins or wheelie bins, put the sacks inside these. Put the lids back on the bins.**

● **Check if there are any rules about what you can put out. Some councils won't collect garden refuse – that's things like grass cuttings, weeds and plants. You have to get special bags for these or take them to the public rubbish tip.**

● **Check that the rubbish has been collected. Has anything been spilt or left behind? You need to clear this up.**

● **If you leave rotting bags of rubbish all over the pavement you could find yourself in trouble with neighbours – or even the council, who can fine you.**

Recycling

Recycling is a great way to help the planet. It cuts down on pollution in the atmosphere. Things made from glass, aluminium and cardboard can often be used to make new products.

Most streets now have a recycling collection as well as a general rubbish collection. The council will give you a plastic bag to collect paper and newspapers for recycling and a plastic box for any rubbish that has the recycling symbol on it.

This will include things like tin cans, plastic drinks bottles, cereal packets and shampoo bottles. Make sure that you rinse out bottles, cans and jars with water before putting them in the recycling box as the council will only collect clean items. And if you don't your box may start to smell and attract flies!

HELPFUL HINT

Make a note of which day your rubbish and recycling are collected and make sure you put it out the night before. Don't wait until the morning – you'll probably oversleep or be in too much of a rush.

Gardening

MOWING THE LAWN

Growing things

Growing plants can be fun – houseplants will make your house look nice and you could even grow fruit or vegetables outside. Whether you're lucky enough to have a garden or you're growing things in window boxes, it's important to look after your green friends.

Outdoor plants

The two things plants need in order to survive are sunlight and water. For most of the year plants growing outside will get all the water they need from the rain. During the summer you may need to water some of them, especially any that are planted in pots.

To water plants use a watering can or a hosepipe. If you use a hosepipe it's best to make sure it has a sprinkler head on the end so that the water does not hit the plants too hard and damage them. Always water the roots of the plants. That's the best way to make sure you don't flatten them!

Houseplants

Houseplants normally need watering about once a week during the spring and summer, and once a fortnight during the winter, but don't swamp them with water or they'll rot! The best thing to do is to press the soil gently with one finger and see if it feels damp. If it is still damp the plant does not need any more water.

Signs of over or under-watering are:

- **leaves dropping off the plant**
- **the plant looks limp and lifeless**
- **the stems and leaves start to rot**

During the spring and summer months (April to September) plants like to be given some extra food. You can buy plant food at most supermarkets and garden centres. Usually, you put a few drops into a container of water and use this to water the plants. But **always read the instructions** or you could end up killing the plant!

Garden chores

Using a lawnmower

Before plugging the lawnmower in (if it is an electric mower), check and do the following:

1 Check that the blade is not clogged up with grass cuttings, as this will stop it working properly.

2 Check the cable is securely connected to the mower.

3 Check the cable has no cuts/damage to it. If it has *you must not use it* because you could electrocute yourself.

4 Make sure the cable is fixed securely into the plug and that the plug is not hanging off the end with the wires showing. Check that the wire is connected to the plug securely (you need to make sure that no stray threads of wire are showing, and that the plastic casing on the outside of the wire slots neatly into the plug). Plug the mower into the circuit breaker, and then into an outdoor extension lead (if the last bit is necessary).

Once you have done the above:

1 Hold the wire away from the mower, turn the mower on and walk in straight lines up and down the lawn until the whole area has been mown.

2 You may need to empty the grass cuttings occasionally if your mower collects them. There's usually a metal/plastic container that you can take off the mower. You may need to switch off the mower to do this.

3 If your mower does not collect the cuttings, you will need to rake them up. Either put them on a compost heap (area where garden refuse rots down to make fertiliser) or bag them up and take them to a rubbish dump.

4 When you have finished, switch off. Then clean all the grass cuttings off the mower and wind up the lead carefully so it will be ready for use next time.

HELPFUL HINT

Switch off the mower when you are doing anything with the blade. If grass or twigs get stuck in it, switch off straight away. Only switch on again when everything is removed. This way you won't chop off your fingers by mistake!

Weeding

You will need:

- A pair of gardening gloves (or any type of thick, tough gloves which will protect your hands properly. You can get these cheaply from DIY and pound shops).

- A small hand trowel or fork.

- Something to collect the weeds in, like a bucket or bin bag.

HELPFUL HINT

Gardening is something you learn from other people, from looking at gardening books and watching gardening programmes on TV and from spending time in your garden. If you're not sure whether something is a weed or plant, leave it where it is! The best thing is to ask someone who knows about gardening to walk around the garden with you and to tell you what things are.

What to do in an emergency

IN THIS SECTION:

In an emergency, don't panic! Stay calm and do something sensible. This chapter will tell you what and how.

Hopefully you won't have to deal with an emergency, but if you do the best thing is to be prepared. If you know where things like fire escapes are, and where to turn the water off, then it's a lot easier to find them in an emergency.

REMEMBER – WHAT YOU DO IN AN EMERGENCY COULD SAVE SOMEONE'S LIFE!

Making emergency phone calls

If you need to call for the **POLICE, AMBULANCE**, or **FIRE BRIGADE in an EMERGENCY...**

DIAL 999

Don't use this number unless it's a real emergency (otherwise the line gets blocked up with calls that aren't urgent, which means someone might die because help doesn't get to them in time).

Emergency	Not an emergency
Someone has fallen down the stairs and is unconscious	You've got a nasty dose of 'flu (call the doctor)
There's a violent fight going on and people are using knives	You noticed someone a bit suspicious hanging round the corner shop (phone the local police)
The house is on fire	You set fire to a chip pan but put it out safely using a fire blanket (read the section on fire blankets)

What you need to do when you dial 999:

1   When you dial 999 the person who answers will ask you which emergency service you require (this means fire, police or ambulance). Think carefully. What is the problem and who do you need? It is vital that you get this right.

2   You will also be asked where you are. If you are at someone's house or in a building, you need to give the address. If you are outside, then give the name of the road you are in. Think of the best way to describe where you are and any landmarks that will

help someone else find you, such as big buildings, parks or supermarkets close by, e.g. 'We are halfway along North Street – opposite the library'.

3   The person on the phone will tell you how long it will be before the emergency service gets to you. Stay where you are and keep calm.

4   If the person on the phone asks you to do something, listen carefully and do exactly as they say. If you are not sure, check again what they want you to do. If necessary, write down the instructions.

HELPFUL HINT

If someone is badly hurt it's usually better not to move them because you may cause them more injury. Try to get advice from 999 first. However, there may be times when you have no choice because you must move them to safety, e.g. there's a fire or they're in a vehicle that might blow up.

 LEE'S STORY

You think it's never going to happen – then it does. It was just me and Angie in the house. She was in the kitchen and I heard her screaming and screaming. When I got in there she'd cut her hand right down to the bone – she'd somehow slipped with this carving knife in her hand. I just stood there for a moment and watched the blood going everywhere. Then I got this towel and wrapped it round her hand as tight as I could. And I rang 999. The woman I spoke to told me how to wrap her hand properly to stop the bleeding. They told me how to keep Angie a bit calmer until the ambulance arrived. It was brilliant having that person to help me.

Fire exits and plans

THE MOST IMPORTANT THING TO DO IN A FIRE IS TO GET OUT OF THE BUILDING.

It is very important you know how to get out of your house if there is a fire. Some buildings have fire escapes which take you out through a special door or staircase, but most ordinary houses don't, so you need to work out your own fire escape plan.

You need to think about:

1   **How many different ways are there to get out of your home? Think about where the doors and windows lead to and where the staircases are.**

2   **How would you get out if you were trapped upstairs?**

3   **How would you get out if you were trapped downstairs?**

4   **Are there any windows that lead on to flat roofs, or which are close enough to the ground that you could use in an emergency?**

5   **If any of these windows are locked, can you unlock them or get to the key easily?**

> **HELPFUL HINT**
>
> **Once you have worked out your escape routes, write them down or draw them clearly on a piece of paper. Pin this somewhere where everyone can see it.**

Using fire extinguishers

There are different coloured fire extinguishers for different types of fires. In your home you should have at least one **fire extinguisher upstairs** (usually on the landing) and one **downstairs** (usually in the kitchen). You should also have a fire blanket kept near the cooker.

The best type of fire extinguishers to have at home are **powder** filled ones because they can be used on most types of fires.

Types of fire extinguishers

These are the different types of fire extinguishers that you can get to use on different kinds of fires.

IT IS IMPORTANT THAT THE RIGHT KIND OF FIRE EXTINGUISHER IS USED ON THE RIGHT KIND OF FIRE OR IT CAN MAKE THE FIRE WORSE!

 DRY CHEMICAL/ POWDER HALON Multi purpose

 WATER electrical equipment, wood and paper

 CARBON DIOXIDE liquids and electrical

A POWDER FIRE EXTINGUISHER CAN BE USED ON ALL TYPES OF FIRES.

HELPFUL HINT

FIRE EXTINGUISHERS ARE NOT TOYS AND SHOULD NEVER BE PLAYED WITH. Playing with a fire extinguisher could damage it and then it would not work if it was needed in a fire. Someone could die because of this.

How to use a fire extinguisher

USE UPRIGHT PULL OUT SAFETY CLIP

STAND BACK 2 METRES AIM AT THE BASE

SQUEEZE THE LEVER AND SWEEP FROM SIDE TO SIDE OF THE FIRE

Using a fire blanket

Every kitchen should have a fire blanket in it somewhere near the cooker. (If you don't have one, ask your landlord about this.)

Fire blankets are designed to be used on cooking fires, such as when a chip pan or toaster catches alight.

- **Fire blankets are good to use on flat pan fires on the cooker or for wrapping around someone whose clothes are on fire.**

- **They are ideal to keep in the kitchen, but they are also good for use in other parts of the house.**

- **Make sure your fire blanket conforms to (meets) British Standard BS 6565.* There will be a symbol which tells you this on the outside.**

*All equipment that you buy should meet what is called "British Standards". This means that they have been tested to make sure that they are safe and that they work properly. If something you buy, such as electrical equipment or toys, does not have the British Standards symbol on them, it means they may not be safe and should not be used.

What to do in a power cut

A power cut is when the lights and other electric things – like toasters, cooker, microwaves – stop working because the electricity supply has "cut out" or has been cut off by the power station.

Make sure you have a torch in the house, and remember where it is, so you can find it if the lights go off.

1   **If the power goes off the most common reason is because the** *trip switch* **has flicked off. The** *trip switch* **can be found in the** *fuse box*, **which is the place where all the fuses for the electrics in the house are kept.**

2   *Fuse boxes* **are usually found in the hallway, utility room, garage or cupboard under the stairs.**

3   **The** *trip switch* **is the switch that says whether the power is** *on* **or** *off*. **When you flick this switch to ON the power should come back on. If it doesn't then you will need to call a qualified electrician.**

4   The *trip switch* will flick off for a number of reasons, but the most common one is that too many sockets and lights are on in the house, so you may need to turn some things off before you can reset the *trip switch*.

5   Very rarely, the power supply may be cut off by the electricity company. This could be for safety or for maintenance reasons and will not last for long.

NEVER ATTEMPT TO REPAIR ELECTRICS YOURSELF UNLESS YOU ARE TRAINED. THE AMOUNT OF POWER RUNNING THROUGH THE MAINS COULD ELECTROCUTE YOU!

How to turn the water off

If you have a burst pipe (usually when they freeze in winter) or discover any pipe leaking you will need to turn the water off until you can get it repaired.

1   When you first move into a house or flat make sure you know where the *stopcock* is. The stopcock is a kind of tap which turns the water on or off. It is usually under the kitchen sink or in the kitchen somewhere, but in old houses it could be almost anywhere!

2   Use the *stopcock* to turn the water off.

3   When you have turned the water off, run all the taps until no water is coming out to empty the system of water.

4   Remember to turn off the central heating, as there will be no water in the radiators to heat them. If you don't you will seriously damage or break the heating system.

HELPFUL HINT

When the water is back on remember to turn the taps on slowly as the water will burst from the taps and could damage the system.

First aid kits

You should have a basic first aid kit in the house which can be used for minor accidents and injuries, such as small cuts and bruises, and minor insect bites.

You can buy this from most chemists and some supermarkets.

What you need in a first aid kit

A first aid kit (for one person) should have in it:

- **2 triangular bandages (size 96cm x 96cm)**
- **a large dressing (18cm x 18cm)**
- **10 assorted plasters**
- **6 safety pins**
- **2 non-alcoholic wipes**
- **a pair of latex gloves**

You can also include:

- **antiseptic cream/liquid/lotion**
- **cotton wool**
- **any other items you may need if you have a medical condition**

Make sure that you replace anything you use from the first aid kit, so that you have everything you need next time.

> ## HELPFUL HINT
>
> **How much do you know about first aid? Organisations like St John's Ambulance run first aid courses all over the UK. For information about a first aid course in your area look on their website at www.sja.org.uk. This website also has downloadable fact sheets on first aid.**

Emergency contact numbers

It is a good idea to keep a list of emergency contact numbers somewhere noticeable so that you – or someone else – can find it in a hurry.

This list should include phone numbers for:

- Your local police station
- Your doctor
- Any other medical person you might need in an emergency, e.g. your specialist
- A close friend/carer/family member (it's a good idea to let these people know that they are on your emergency list)
- Your social worker or key worker
- A plumber
- An electrician
- The gas board

5

Your rights and the law

Your rights

IN THIS SECTION:

This chapter tells you about the law and your rights. You might not want to read it all in one go, but the information is here when you need to check something.

What the law says

If you are a young person leaving care, the Children (Leaving Care) Act 2000 lists what services you are entitled to.* Your local authority must give you access to these services, and make sure you continue to receive support. The law says that, if you are between the ages of 16 and 21, you should be 'prepared for ceasing to be looked after' ('ceasing' is another word for ending or finishing). Your local authority must 'advise, assist and befriend' you in order to 'promote' your welfare in the future.

*At the time this guide was published the law only applied to England and Wales, but similar laws are being introduced in Scotland and Northern Ireland.

Your Personal Adviser

The Children (Leaving Care) Act 2000 says that your local authority should provide you with a Personal Adviser. This person is responsible for 'assessing' your needs and deciding what 'advice, assistance and support' they should give you to help you prepare for the future. As part of this, your Personal Advisor will work with you to prepare a 'Pathway Plan'.

Pathway Plans

Your Pathway Plan will map out what your needs are, and how they will be met. It should be regularly reviewed to make sure it is still right for you. Your Pathway Plan will include where you are going to live, and your plans for education or training, or getting a job. The Plan will also say when the local authority thinks you will no longer need support from them or your Personal Adviser.

Your Personal Adviser will also know about grants and funds of money that will help you when you are setting up your home, or need things for college or your job. They will apply for these on your behalf.

There are also some services which all young people – whether they are in care or not – may come across as they prepare for adult life. These include things like career advice and help with health and personal issues.

Financial support

Your local authority has certain financial responsibilities for you. The law says that young people of 16 or 17 cannot receive state benefits (like housing benefit and unemployment benefit) unless they are disabled or a single parent. Instead, your local authority gives you a living allowance. This should never be less money than the amount you would have received if you were allowed to claim benefits.

Once you reach 18, you are expected to pay for your own living costs. If you are not working or do not earn enough, you can get state benefits to help with these costs. Your local authority must also help you with the costs of education, training and things you may need to get a job up to the age of 21. If you are in full-time education, e.g. going to college or university, then this help will continue until you are 24. Your local authority must also find or pay for somewhere for you to live during the holidays if you live in college or university accommodation during term time.

You may get extra help with costs such as:

● **Buying books and equipment for education/training**

● **Travelling to college or training**

● **Buying smart clothes for interviews or protective clothing for your job**

● **Going on a holiday**

● **Following a hobby, e.g. the fee to join your local gym**

● **Following your religion or things which are important in your culture, such as special foods or clothes**

● **Staying in touch with members of your family or other important people in your life**

● **Counselling or other specialist services to help you cope with difficult experiences**

Your Personal Adviser will explain your options and help you to think about the ones which apply to you. They will write in your Pathway Plan which payments you will receive.

Unaccompanied asylum seekers

If you came into this country as an unaccompanied asylum seeker then you are the responsibility of the local authority up to the age of 18. By the time you are 18 the Home Office should reach a decision as to whether you will be allowed to remain in the country. If this is not decided by the time you reach 18, you will not be entitled to receive state benefits while you wait for this decision. Your local authority must apply for special government funding to support you.

Legal age guide – your basic rights

At any age you can:

● Have an account opened in your name with a bank or building society. Providing they think you understand the nature of transactions, you can operate the account yourself. Under 18s cannot have an overdraft.

● Have a passport of your own if a parent/guardian signs the application form. Under the age of five years, provision of a passport is at the discretion of the Passport Office.

● Be subject to a care order until you reach the age of 18.

● Have premium bonds in your name.

● Consent to or refuse surgical, medical or dental treatment, provided you understand the nature of the decision. This also applies to contraceptive treatment (but see 'From age 16').

● See a "U" or "PG" film with permission from your parent/guardian.

From age 5 you can:

● Drink alcohol legally in private (but it is illegal for anyone to sell alcohol for consumption by any person under 18 except in a restaurant to over 16s for consumption with a meal).

- Become of "compulsory school age"

From age 7 you can:

- Draw money from a Post Office account

From age 8 you can:

- Be found guilty of a crime or offence (Scotland only)

From age 10 you can (England and Wales):

- Be convicted of a criminal offence, if it is proved that you knew the difference between right and wrong

- Be remanded in care to await trial

- Be fingerprinted, photographed, searched or subjected to an intimate search. From age 10–13, your parent/guardian's consent must be given in most cases for fingerprinting, photographing, or for intimate searches. However, in certain circumstances this can be done without your parent/guardian's consent. If you are cleared of the offence or if you are not prosecuted/cautioned, the fingerprint sample must be destroyed. This also applies if you are not a suspect (i.e. if you are a victim).

From age 12 you can:

- See a "12" certificate film

- Buy a pet animal

From age 13 you can:

- Be employed for a certain number of hours a week, for example, outside school hours between 7am and 7pm, for not more than two hours on school days or a Sunday. The work must not be of a "heavy" nature.

- Work up to five hours per day on Saturday and in school holidays (provided you do not work more than 25 hours per week)

From age 14 you can:

- Be held fully responsible for a crime

- Go into a pub, but not to drink alcohol there

- If you're a boy you can be convicted of rape, assault with intent to commit rape and unlawful sexual intercourse with a girl under 16

- If you're a boy you can be sent to a Young Offenders institution for a maximum of four months

From age 15 you can:

- See a "15" certificate film

- Be sent to a Young Offenders institution for a maximum of 12 months

- Work up to eight hours per day on Saturdays and in school holidays (no more than 35 hours per week)

From age 16 you can:

- Get a National Insurance number

- Claim certain benefits in your own right

- Buy Premium Bonds

- Buy cigarettes or tobacco

- Join a trade union. Some unions will allow you to join before you are 16.

- Leave school

- Choose your own doctor, and consent to medical, surgical or dental treatment, without your parent/guardian's consent

- Work full time

- Pay prescription charges (certain people are exempt, for example, if you are unemployed, on a low income, or in full-time education up to age 19)

- Consent to sexual intercourse

- A young man can join the Armed Forces with his parent/guardian's permission

- Probably leave home without your parent/guardian's consent, but you may be subject to a care order or wardship

- Get married with your parent/guardian's or the Court's consent

- Drink wine or beer in a restaurant with a meal
- Help collect charitable donations
- Buy fireworks
- Hold a licence to drive a moped, motorcycle, certain tractors or invalid carriages
- Apply for help with legal costs
- Be given a Community Service Order if you are found guilty of a criminal offence
- In certain limited circumstances be able to apply for Income Support

From age 17 you can:

- Hold a licence to drive any vehicle except certain heavy ones
- Be sent to a remand centre to await trial
- Become a street trader
- Appear before an adult court if charged with an offence
- If you're a girl you can join the Armed Forces with your parent/guardian's consent
- A Probation Order can be made on you

From age 18 you can:

- Leave home without your parent/guardian's consent
- Get married without your parent/guardian's consent
- Vote in a parliamentary election
- Get a tattoo
- Act as an executor of a person's will
- See an "18" film
- Enter a betting shop and bet
- Change your name
- Make a will

- Apply for a passport without your parent/guardian's consent
- Own houses and land
- Sue and be sued
- Go abroad to sing, play or perform professionally without a licence
- Sit on a jury
- Be a blood donor
- Buy alcohol
- Drink alcohol in a pub
- Pawn an article in a pawn shop
- Apply for a mortgage (but most building societies will not consider applicants under 21 years of age)
- If you are adopted, you can see your birth certificate on application to the Registrar General

From age 21 you can:

- Stand in a parliamentary or local election
- Drive any mechanically propelled vehicle
- Hold a licence to sell alcohol
- Adopt a child

The law

IN THIS SECTION:

'What me, officer? I was nowhere near at the time.'

The law is there to protect you. Make sure you stay on the right side of it and benefit from its protection.

There are various ways you can get involved with the law.

- **Getting the help of the law, e.g. if you are burgled, attacked or have your purse stolen**

- **Upholding the law – by reporting a crime or giving evidence to help the police catch someone who has broken the law**

- **Breaking the law, e.g. shoplifting, drunk driving, drug dealing, public order offences, etc**

Getting the help of the law

If you are the victim of a crime you should dial 999 (in an emergency) or contact your local police station.

If you have been burgled try not to touch or move things. The police may need to "finger print" things the burglars may have touched.

While you are waiting for the police to arrive, try to remember as many details as you can. What has been stolen? Make a list of the things that were in your room, in your bag or wallet.

Some other reasons you might need the help of the law include:

- **You are the victim of domestic violence or worried about someone else whom this is happening to**

- **You are worried that a child is being abused or neglected**

- **You or someone else has been attacked or raped**

- **You are the victim of racist crime**

- **You have lost something valuable**

- **Someone has taken money from you by using your bank account**

- **You have lost your dog or you have found a stray dog**

- **You want to report an "abandoned vehicle" which is creating an eyesore in your street**

- **You want to report something which happened in the past – which you only now feel strong enough to talk about**

Upholding the law

You might witness something like an accident, an assault or a burglary. You may be asked by the police to give a statement to describe what you have seen. You may be asked to attend a court hearing to describe to the court what you have seen and heard.

If you know about a crime but are worried about reporting this, you can call Crimestoppers on 0800 555 111. You don't have to give your name.

Breaking the law (don't do it!)

Getting into trouble with the law isn't a good idea. You might end up being taken to court and getting fined or imprisoned.

People with criminal convictions can find it harder to get jobs. You may have to declare a conviction if you apply for certain jobs. (Some convictions are considered to be "spent" after a period of time but for some jobs you will always have to declare a previous conviction.)

If you have committed crimes when you were younger and have had a reprimand or warning from a court (rather than a conviction), this should not affect your chance of getting a job in the future – so long as you do not commit further crimes.

Anti-Social Behaviour Orders

The Government introduced something called Anti-Social Behaviour Orders – ASBOs – recently. If someone gets an ASBO, it is designed to stop any anti-social behaviour or act that they might have carried out, rather than punishing the person who has done this. ASBOs can be imposed on young people if a young person is seen to be behaving in ways which cause harassment, alarm or distress. Some examples of behaviour or acts that could result in a young person getting an ASBO are as follows:

- **Spraying graffiti on walls**
- **Using abusive language**
- **Excessive noise, particularly late at night**
- **Throwing rubbish and litter on the streets**

- Drunken behaviour in the streets and the mess it creates
- Dealing drugs, and all the problems this creates

These are issues which concern everyone in the community – young and old.

Some young people see ASBOs as a kind of badge of honour, but don't be fooled! If you get an ASBO, you may not be able to go out to certain places at certain times, or see a particular group of friends.

An ASBO won't go on your criminal record – but if you get one and breach it, this is a criminal offence and you could get sent to prison or be fined.

TONY'S STORY

I used to think it was cool to be bad. It's all about reputation. The badder you are, the more reputation you get. The more reputation you get, the less likely anyone will mess around with you as you walk down the street. I only started being antisocial when I was 16. Now I'm seeing kids as young as 13 being antisocial.

I did petty stuff like stealing from shops and joining groups where our friends would steal a Vespa and I would take a ride on it, but we didn't attack anyone or slap people for no reason. We were having a laugh in this building one day and I was arrested for having a screwdriver on me. I ended up going to court for it and it went on for ages. I got off with a slap on the wrist but I stopped hanging out with the other guys and moved on to college.

(Taken from *The Guardian G2*, 4 August 2006)

Avoiding trouble

Don't put yourself in a situation where you could end up on the wrong side of the law.

- Don't get involved in other people's arguments and fights.

- If someone challenges you, don't provoke the situation by your actions. Think carefully about what would be a good course of action for you to take to keep yourself safe and out of trouble.

- Sometimes walking away is the best thing to do. Let them call you names – it's less painful than getting broken bones.

- Avoid breaking rules such as drinking alcohol in "Alcohol free zones".

- Make sure you pay your way, for example, buying tickets when you travel on trains and buses. Make sure you pay all your bills as legal action can be taken against you in some cases. You may also be "black-listed" which means you will be unable to get some services in the future.

- If you get a fine or penalty, e.g. for parking in the wrong place, don't ignore it. You can get taken to court for not paying fines.

Keeping things cool

If you do find yourself in trouble with the police, don't make the situation worse. Follow these basic rules:

- If the police approach you in the street while you are very drunk and tell you to calm down and stop doing something, it's a good idea to do what they say.

Don't get into an argument and don't swear at the police. If you do you could end up in a police cell.

- If the police "flag you down" while you are driving, don't play car chases. Pull over. If you know you've done something wrong – like speeding – it's often better to admit it and apologise. You stand a better chance of being let off with a warning. If you are rude or aggressive, you are more likely to get a fine or a court summons.

- If you are arrested for a crime, don't struggle or fight with the police. Go calmly. Otherwise you can make things more uncomfortable for yourself and get extra charges added to what they're arresting you for.

If you are arrested

● Ask for a solicitor (you are entitled to this, free of charge).

● If you are under 18 you are entitled to the support of an "appropriate adult". This person could be a family member, foster carer or someone else you know and trust. Social services can also provide an appropriate adult if you have no adult to call on. This person makes sure your rights are protected, that you are fairly treated and that you don't feel on your own.

● It's often best to wait until you have someone with you before you answer any questions.

Useful organisations

The Children's Legal Centre
University of Essex
Wivenhoe Park
Colchester CO4 3SQ
Freephone: 0800 783 2187
www.childrenslegalcentre.com
Lots of info on children's and young people's rights and the law as it affects children and young people.

The BBC's website, **www.bbc.co.uk**, has a wealth of information about all sorts of subjects. This includes legal advice for young people.

Visit **www.womensaid.org.uk** for advice and information on domestic violence.

www.cjsonline.gov.uk has a virtual "walkthrough" of the Criminal Justice System which is helpful for anyone who is being a witness, a juror, is the victim of a crime or is being tried for a crime.

For details about **Crimestoppers** – the UK-wide charity dedicated to stopping crime – visit www.crimestoppers-uk.org.

6

Useful addresses

Useful names, addresses and organisations

General help and advice

Albert Kennedy Trust

Runs schemes to find foster carers, lodgings and housing for lesbian, gay and bisexual young people.
Unit 305a Hatton Square
16/16a Baldwin Gardens
London EC1N 7RJ
Tel: 020 7831 6562
www.akt.org.uk

Care for Life

A Christian charity which provides a number of social caring and educational projects for young people.
53 Romney Street
London SW1P 3RF
Tel: 020 7233 0455
www.care.org.uk

Childline

A free and confidential 24-hour helpline for children and young people.
45 Folgate Street
London E1 6GL
Freephone: 0800 1111
www.childline.org.uk

Children's Legal Centre

Provides legal advice and information to children, young people and their carers.
University of Essex
Wivenhoe Park
Colchester CO4 3SQ
Freephone: 0800 783 2187
www.childrenslegalcentre.com

Citizens Advice Bureaux

Provides free, independent information and advice on legal, money and other problems.
Myddleton House
115–123 Pentonville Road
London N1 9LZ
Tel: 020 7833 2181
www.citizensadvice.org.uk

Connexions

Offers advice on education, careers, housing, money and health for 13–19-year-olds.
Freephone: 0808 001 3219
www.connexions.gov.uk

Crimestoppers

Works to help identify, prevent, solve and reduce crime. Anyone can contact them anonymously to report details of crime.
Freephone: 0800 555 111
www.crimestoppers-uk.org

Cruse

Provides bereavement care for anyone who has been affected by a death.
Cruse House
126 Sheen Road
Richmond TW1 1UR
Freephone: 0808 808 1677
www.crusebereavementcare.org.uk

Eating Disorders Association
Provides information and advice
on all aspects of eating
disorders.
103 Prince of Wales Road
Norwich NR1 1DW
Tel: 0845 634 7650
4.30pm–8.30pm Mon–Fri
Youthline for under 19s
www.edauk.com

Lesbian and Gay Switchboard
A 24-hour helpline offering
support, advice and information
to lesbians, gay men and
bisexuals.
Tel: 020 7837 7324
www.llgs.org.uk

MIND
Works to advance the views and
needs of people with mental
health problems, and provides
advice and support.
15–19 Broadway
London E15 4BQ
Tel: 0845 766 0163
9.15am–5.15pm Mon–Fri
www.mind.org.uk

**NACRO (National Association for
the Care and Resettlement of
Offenders)**
Helps ex-offenders and their
families to improve their lives
and futures.
169 Clapham Road
London SW9 0PU
Tel: 020 7582 6500
www.nacro.org.uk

National Debt Line
Provides free, confidential and
independent advice on dealing
with debt problems.
Tricorn House
51–53 Hagley Road
Edgbaston
Birmingham B16 8TP
Freephone: 0808 080 4000
www.nationaldebtline.co.uk

Shelter
Provides a 24-hour national
housing service.
88 Old Street
London EC1V 9HU
Freephone: 0808 800 4444
www.shelter.org.uk

Rape Crisis Centre
Look in Yellow Pages under 'R'
for your local branch.

Refuge
Provides a 24-hour domestic
violence helpline for women and
children, and a network of safe
houses.
Freephone: 0808 200 0247
www.refuge.org.uk

Refugee Council
Offers help and support to
asylum seekers and refugees.
240–250 Ferndale Road
London SW9 8BB
Tel: 020 7346 6700
www.refugeecouncil.org.uk

Women's Aid
Works to end domestic violence
against women and children, and
provides help and advice.
Head Office
PO Box 391
Bristol BS99 7WS
Freephone: 0808 200 0247
www.womensaid.org.uk

Sexual health and pregnancy

Brook Advisory Centre
Provides confidential sexual
health advice and free
contraception to young people up
to the age of 25.
421 Highgate Studios
53–79 Highgate Road
London NW5 1TL
Freephone:0800 018 5023
Helpline: 0800 292 930
                    advice for under 19s

FPA
(Family Planning Association)
Offers help, advice and
information on contraception and
sexual health.
50 Featherstone Street
London EC1Y 8QU
Tel: 0845 310 1334
9am–6pm Mon–Fri
www.fpa.org.uk

National AIDS Helpline
A 24-hour helpline for anyone
affected by AIDS.
Freephone: 0800 567 123

Terrence Higgins Trust
Provides advice and information
on HIV and AIDS.
314–320 Gray's Inn Road
London WC1X 8DP
Tel: 0845 122 1200
10am–10pm Mon–Fri
12noon–6pm Sat–Sun
www.tht.org.uk/

Drugs and alcohol

Adfam
Offers confidential support for families and friends of drug users.
Tel: 020 7553 7640
www.adfam.org.uk

Alateen and Al-Anon Family Groups
Services for young people and families who think they may have a drinking problem or are worried about someone close to them.
Tel: 020 7403 0888
10am–10pm
www.al-anonuk.org.uk

Alcoholics Anonymous
A service for anyone who thinks they may have a drinking problem.
Tel: 0845 769 7555
www.alcoholics-anonymous.org.uk

Drugscope
Provides information on drugs.
32–36 Loman Street
London SE1 0EE
Tel: 020 7928 1211
www.drugscope.org.uk

National Drugs Helpline
Provides information and advice on drugs.
Freephone: 0800 776 600
www.talktofrank.com

Quit
Provides advice, help and information for all those trying to give up smoking.
Ground Floor
211 Old Street
London EC1V 9NR
Freephone: 0800 002 200
www.quit.org.uk

Education, employment and volunteering

Community Service Volunteers
Provides information and organises volunteer projects across the UK.
237 Pentonville Road
London N1 9NJ
Tel: 020 7278 6601
www.csv.org.uk

Open University
PO Box 197
Milton Keynes MK7 6BJ
Tel: 0870 333 4340
www.open.ac.uk

Princes Trust Volunteers
Provides advice and practical support for young people aged 14–30 to realise their potential.
18 Park Square East
London NW1 4LH
Tel: 020 7543 1234
www.princes-trust.org.uk

SKILL
Promotes opportunities for young people with any disability in post-16 education, training and work.
Chapter House
18–20 Crucifix Lane
London SE1 3JW
Freephone: 0800 328 5050
www.skill.org.uk

Voluntary Service Overseas
Organises voluntary work placements overseas.
317 Putney Bridge Road
London SW15 2PN
Tel: 020 8780 7200
www.vso.org.uk

General help and projects for people being fostered or adopted

Barnardo's
Offers a wide range of support services for children, young people and families.
Tanners Lane
Barkingside
Ilford IG6 1QG
Tel: 020 8550 8822
www.barnardos.org.uk

The Children's Society
Provides help and advice for children and young people.
Edward Rudolf House
Margery Street
London WC1X 0JL
Tel: 020 7841 4400
www.the-childrens-society.org.uk

The Fostering Network Young People's Project (England and Wales)
Works with young people on a number of projects aimed at allowing young people's voices to be heard.
87 Blackfriars Road
London SE1 8HA
Tel: 020 7620 6412
www.fostering.net/england/youngpeople.php

The Fostering Network Young People's Project (Scotland)
Second Floor
Ingram House
227 Ingram Street
Glasgow G1 1DA
Tel: 0141 204 1400
www.fostering.net/scotland/young_people/

National Children's Bureau – Young NCB

A free membership network for children and young people aged 17 and under which gives members the chance to speak out on important issues.
8 Wakely Street
London EC1V 7QE
Tel: 020 7843 6000
www.ncb.org.uk
Young NCB:
www.ncb.org.uk/page.asp?sve=786

The Scottish Throughcare and Aftercare Forum

Aims to improve support for young people leaving care in Scotland by consulting with young people and workers.
Second Floor
37 Otago Street
Glasgow G12 8JJ
Tel: 0141 357 4124
www.scottishthroughcare.org.uk/youth/index.asp

Voice
(formerly Voice for the Child in Care)

Works with children and young people in care to support them and promote their views.
Unit 4, Pride Court
80–82 White Lion Street
London N1 9PF
Freephone: 0808 800 5792
www.vcc-uk.org

The Who Cares? Trust

Aims to improve the lives of children and young people in residential and foster care. Runs CareZone, an interactive online network for young people in care.
Kemp House
152–160 City Road
London EC1V 2NP
Tel: 020 7251 3117
www.thewhocarestrust.org.uk
CareZone:
www.thewhocarestrust.org.uk/carezone.htm

My Personal Information

First name(s): ....

Surname: ....

Preferred name if different from above: ....

Date of birth: ....

My National Insurance Number: ....

My address is: ....

....

....

My telephone number is: ....

My mobile number is: ....

My email address is: ....

My birth certificate is kept: ....

My passport number is: ....

My medical registration NHS number is: ....

My doctor's name is: ....

My doctor's address is: ....

....

....

My doctor's telephone number is: ....

My dentist's name is: ....

My optician's name is: ....

My landlord's name is: ....

My school/college address is: ....

....

....

My school/college telephone number is: ....

My tutor's name is: ....

My work address is: ....

....

....

My boss's name is: ....

My social worker's name is: ....

My social worker can be contacted at: ....

My emergency contact is: ....

Useful addresses & telephone numbers

Name ....

Address ....

....

....

Post code ....

Telephone ....

Mobile ....

Email ....

Name ....

Address ....

....

....

Post code ....

Telephone ....

Mobile ....

Email ....

Name ....

Address ....

....

....

Post code ....

Telephone ....

Mobile ....

Email ....

Name ....

Address ....

....

....

Post code ....

Telephone ....

Mobile ....

Email ....

Name ....

Address ....

....

....

Post code ....

Telephone ....

Mobile ....

Email ....

Name ....

Address ....

....

....

Post code ....

Telephone ....

Mobile ....

Email ....

Name ....

Address ....

....

....

Post code ....

Telephone ....

Mobile ....

Email ....

Name ....

Address ....

....

....

Post code ....

Telephone ....

Mobile ....

Email ....

Name ....

Address ....

....

....

Post code ....

Telephone................................

Mobile ....

Email....................................

Name ....

Address ....

....

....

Post code ....

Telephone................................

Mobile ....

Email....................................

Name ....

Address ....

....

....

Post code ....

Telephone................................

Mobile ....

Email....................................

Name ....

Address ....

....

....

Post code ....

Telephone................................

Mobile ....

Email....................................

Name....................................

Address ....

....

....

Post code...............................

Telephone................................

Mobile...................................

Email....................................

Name....................................

Address ....

....

....

Post code...............................

Telephone................................

Mobile...................................

Email....................................

Name....................................

Address ....

....

....

Post code...............................

Telephone................................

Mobile...................................

Email....................................

Name....................................

Address ....

....

....

Post code...............................

Telephone................................

Mobile...................................

Email....................................